Edited by **Ari Yarwood**
Book Design by **Sarah Graley** & **Stef Purenins**

Published by **Oni Press, Inc.**
Joe Nozemack, Founder & Chief Financial Officer × **James Lucas Jones**, Publisher
Sarah Gaydos, Editor in Chief × **Charlie Chu**, V.P. of Creative & Business Development
Brad Rooks, Director of Operations × **Margot Wood**, Director of Sales
Amber O'Neill, Special Projects Manager × **Troy Look**, Director of Design & Production
Kate Z. Stone, Senior Graphic Designer × **Sonja Synak**, Graphic Designer
Angie Knowles, Digital Prepress Lead × **Robin Herrera**, Senior Editor × **Ari Yarwood**, Senior Editor
Michelle Nguyen, Executive Assistant × **Jung Lee**, Logistics Associate

Originally self-published by **Shiny Sword Press**

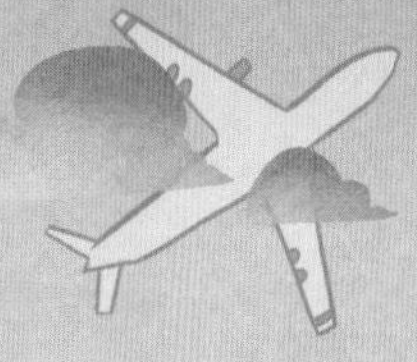

1319 SE Martin Luther King, Jr. Blvd.
Suite 240
Portland, OR 97214

onipress.com
facebook.com/onipress
twitter.com/onipress
onipress.tumblr.com
instagram.com/onipress

oursuperadventure.com
sarahgraley.com
@sarahgraleyart

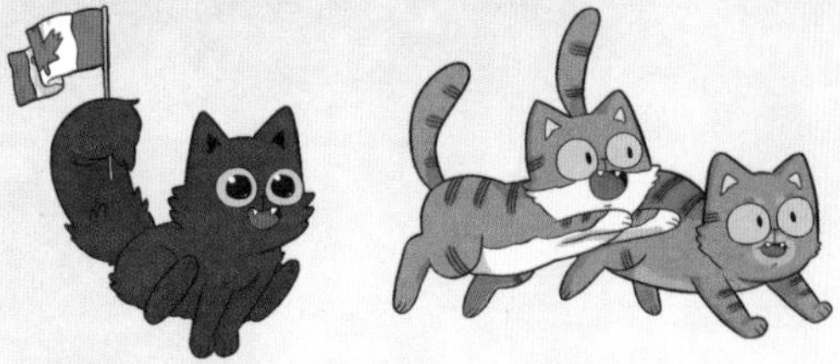

First Edition: November 2019
Retail Edition ISBN: 978-1-62010-673-0 **Artist Edition ISBN:** 978-1-62010-674-7

Printed in China.

Library of Congress Control Number: 2019934125

1 2 3 4 5 6 7 8 9 10

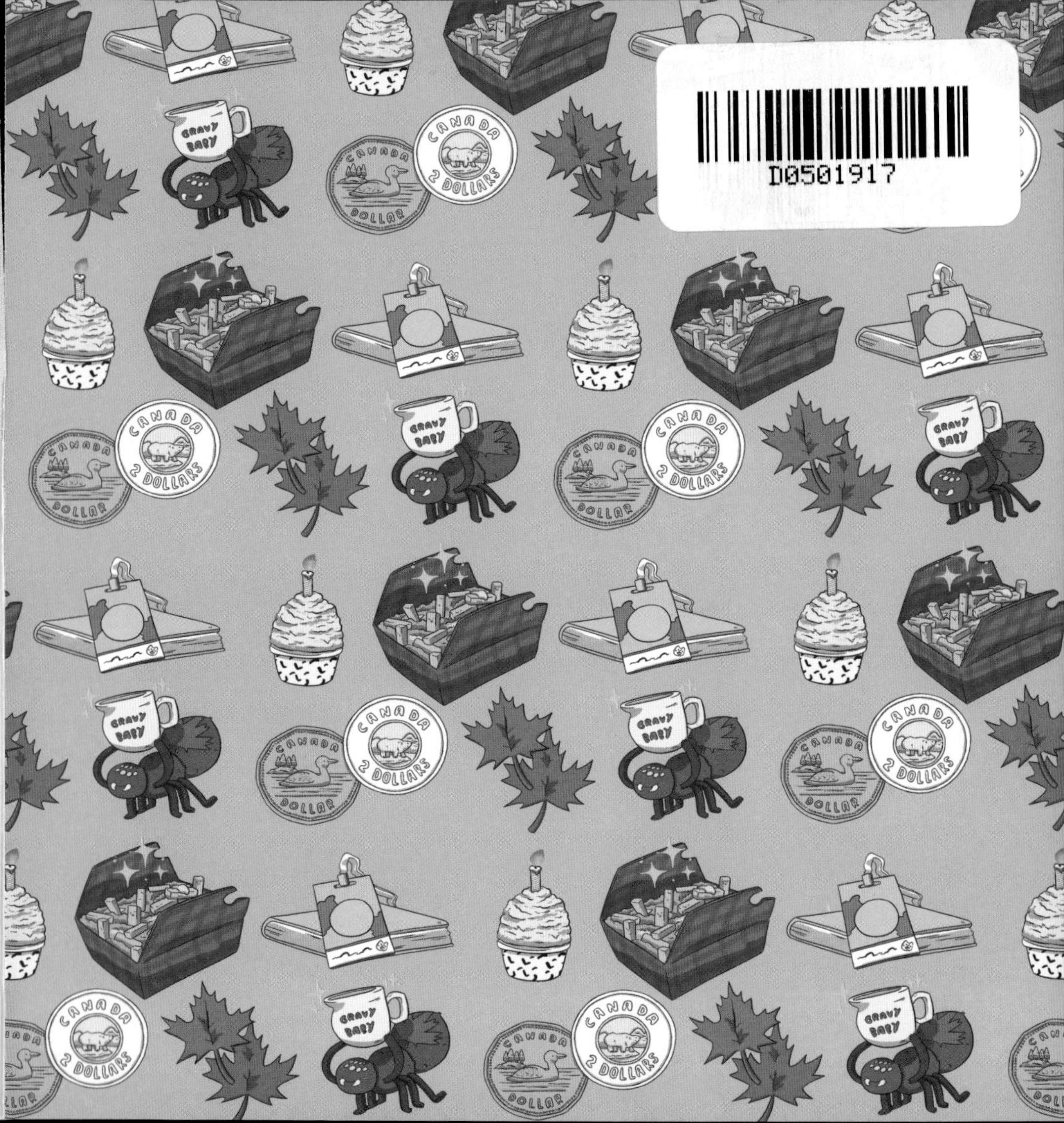
GRAVY BABY
CANADA
2 DOLLARS
CANADA
DOLLAR

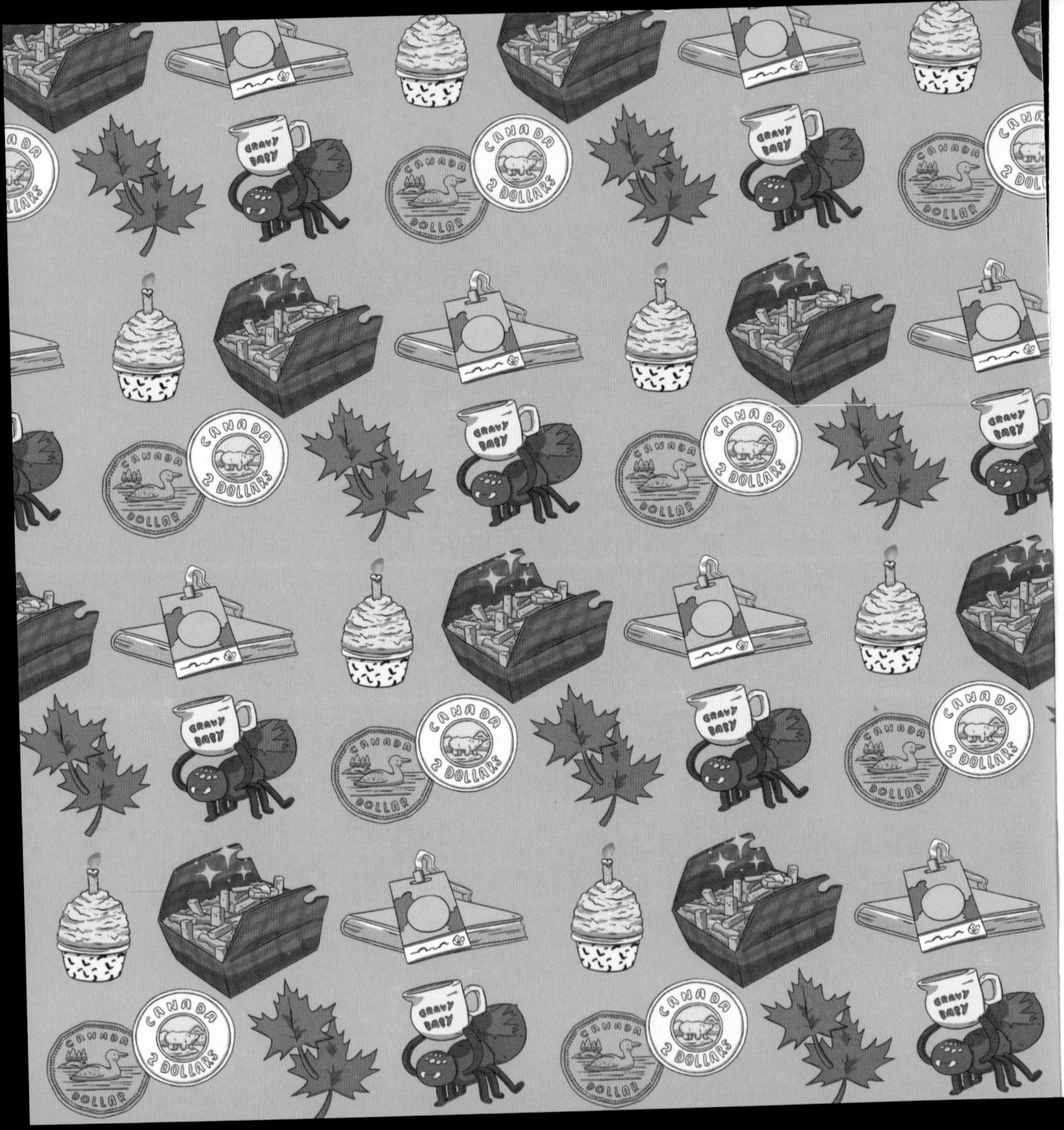
CANADA
DOLLAR
CANADA
2 DOLLARS
GRAVY BABY

OUR SUPER CANADIAN ADVENTURE

AN OUR SUPER ADVENTURE TRAVELOGUE

by Sarah Graley and Stef Purenins

AN ONI PRESS
PUBLICATION

SUPER [A]DIAN ADVENTURE

AN OUR SUPER ADVENTURE TRAVELOGUE

by Sarah Graley and Stef Purenins

Written by **Sarah Graley** and **Stef Purenins**
Art and Colouring by **Sarah Graley**
Lettering, Colour Assisting and Design by **Stef Purenins**

INTRODUCTION

Our Super Canadian Adventure is a travelogue comic that documents our first-ever trip to Canada!

We spent a week in Toronto doing tourist stuff before ending the trip by attending TCAF (Toronto Comic and Arts Festival) for the first time!

Ever since Stef and I started dating (7 years at time of writing!), attending TCAF was always something that we wanted to do, and after we came super close to visiting in 2017 (we ended up moving house around the same time and had to rethink our plans) we were overjoyed to visit in 2018! It's a wonderful comics event that fills the Toronto Reference Library with amazing cartoonists from all over the world - I highly recommend it!

I hope you enjoy this collection of comics! We had the nicest time in Toronto and we honestly can't wait to go back.

- Sarah and Stef

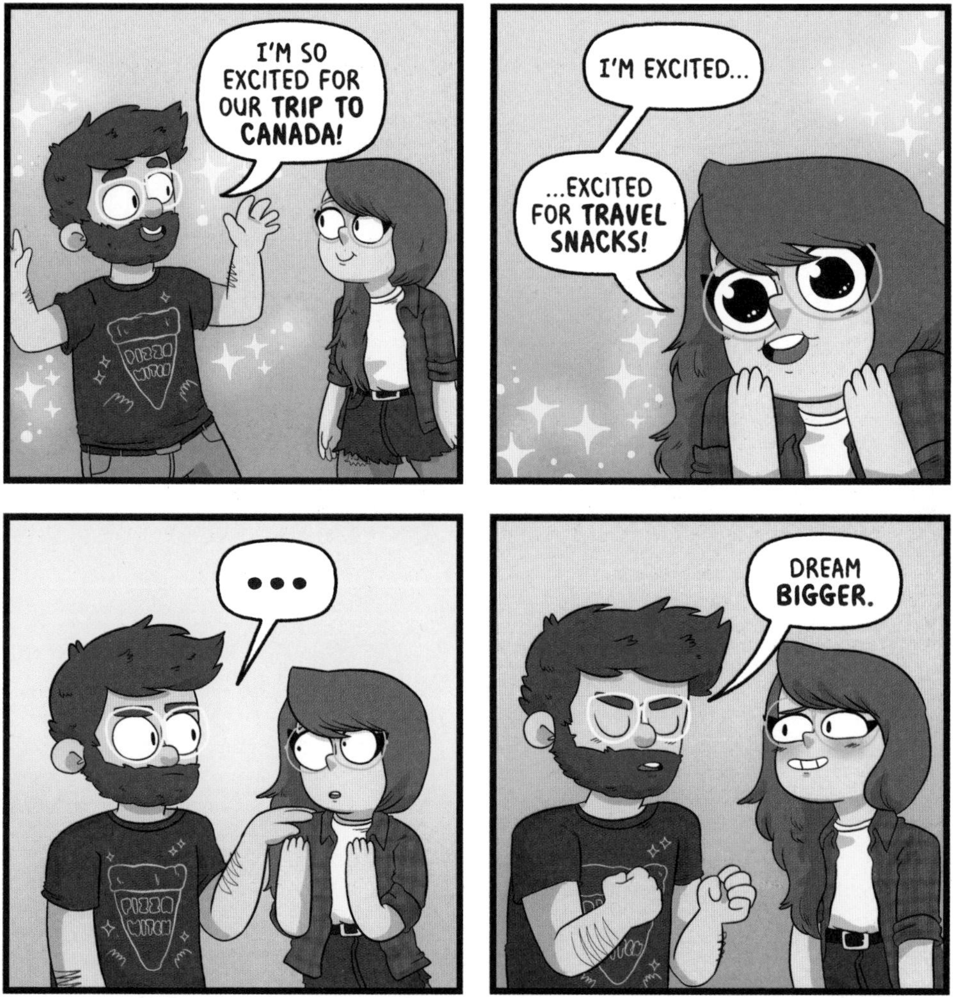
I'M SO EXCITED FOR OUR TRIP TO CANADA!
I'M EXCITED...
...EXCITED FOR TRAVEL SNACKS!
...
DREAM BIGGER.

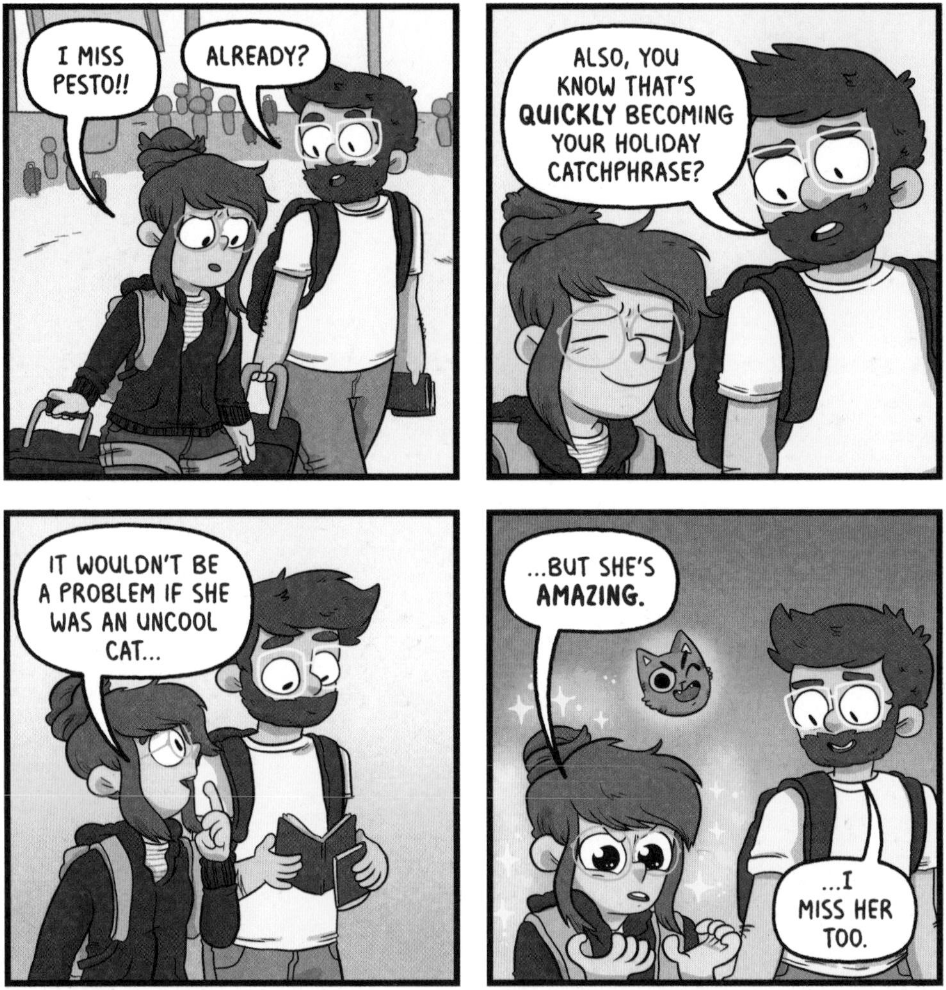
I MISS PESTO!!
ALREADY?
ALSO, YOU KNOW THAT'S **QUICKLY** BECOMING YOUR HOLIDAY CATCHPHRASE?
IT WOULDN'T BE A PROBLEM IF SHE WAS AN UNCOOL CAT...
...BUT SHE'S **AMAZING.**
...I MISS HER TOO.

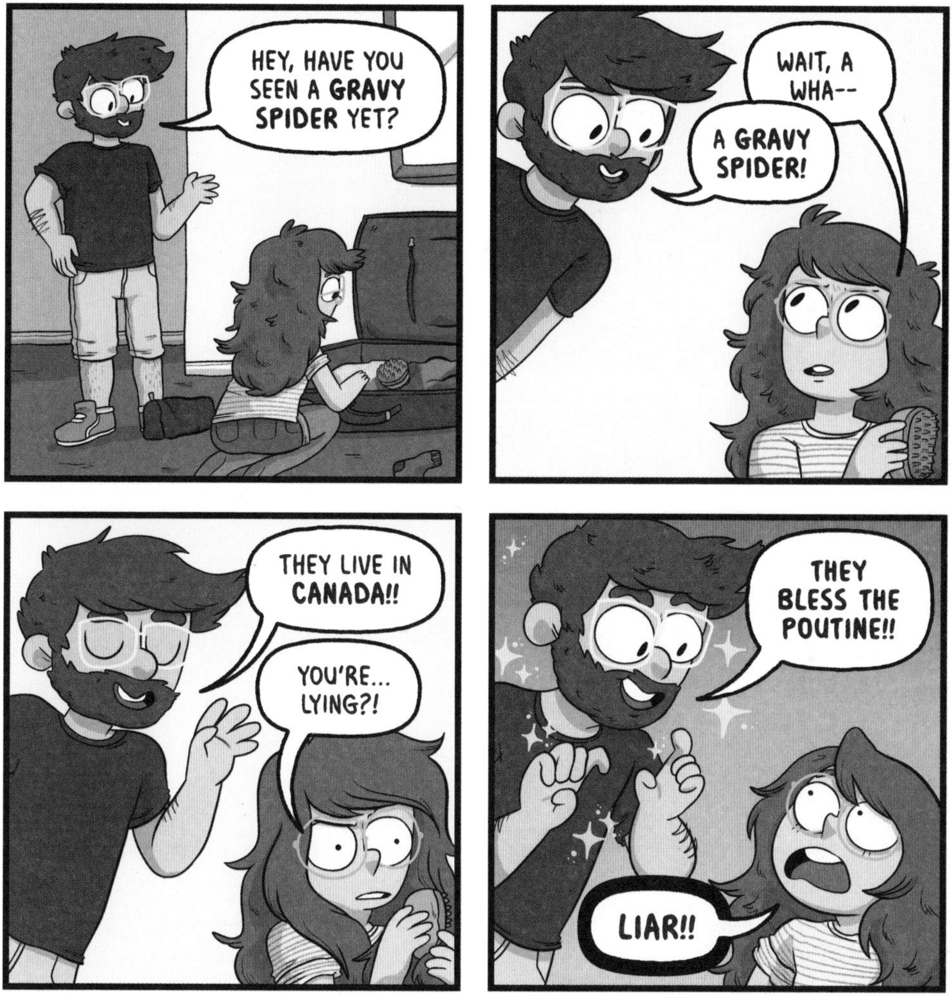
HEY, HAVE YOU SEEN A **GRAVY SPIDER** YET?
WAIT, A WHA--
A **GRAVY SPIDER!**
THEY LIVE IN **CANADA!!**
YOU'RE... LYING?!
THEY BLESS THE POUTINE!!
LIAR!!

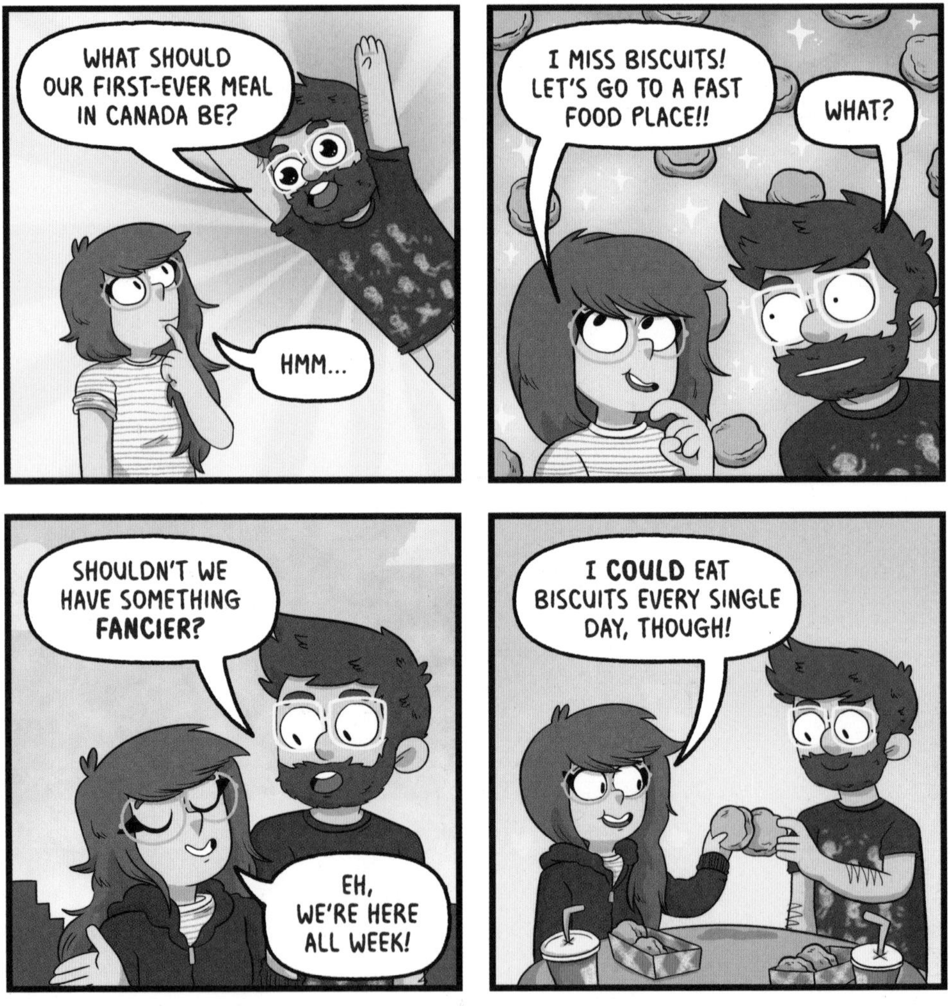
WHAT SHOULD OUR FIRST-EVER MEAL IN CANADA BE?
HMM...
I MISS BISCUITS! LET'S GO TO A FAST FOOD PLACE!!
WHAT?
SHOULDN'T WE HAVE SOMETHING **FANCIER?**
EH, WE'RE HERE ALL WEEK!
I **COULD** EAT BISCUITS EVERY SINGLE DAY, THOUGH!

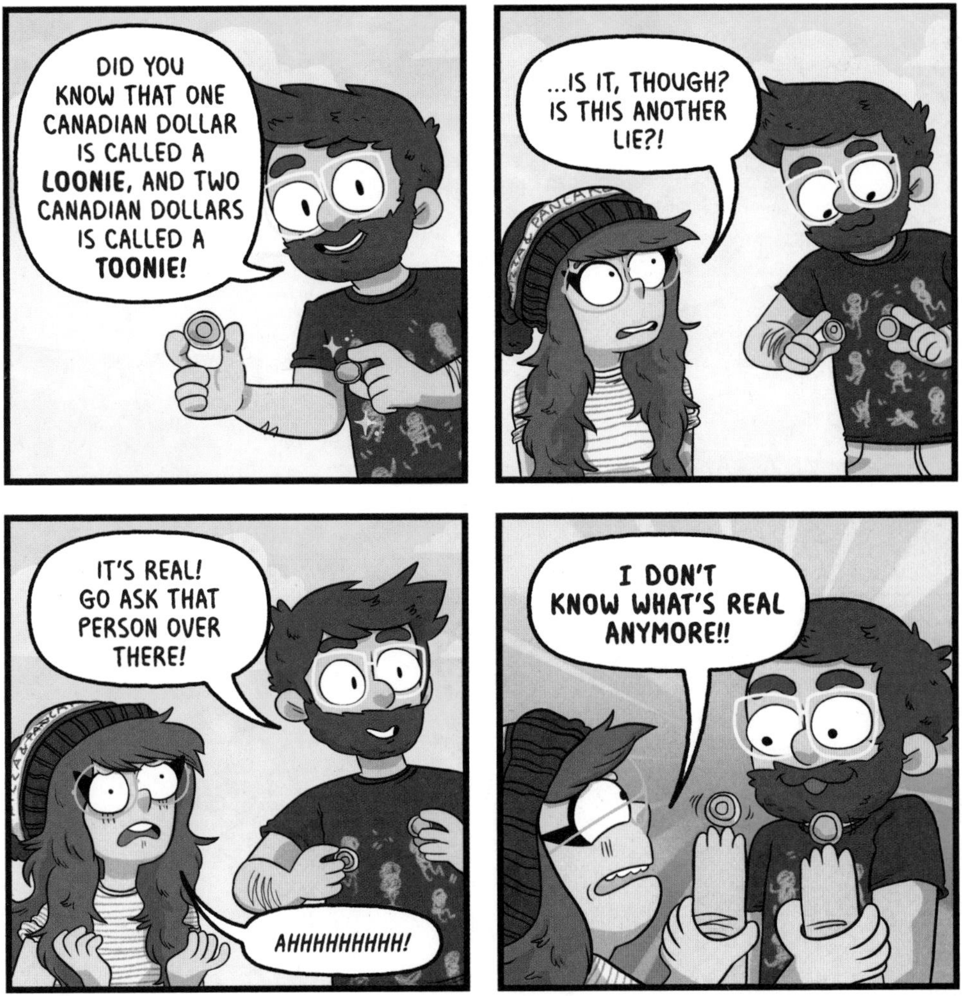
DID YOU KNOW THAT ONE CANADIAN DOLLAR IS CALLED A **LOONIE**, AND TWO CANADIAN DOLLARS IS CALLED A **TOONIE**!
...IS IT, THOUGH? IS THIS ANOTHER LIE?!
IT'S REAL! GO ASK THAT PERSON OVER THERE!
AHHHHHHHHH!
I DON'T KNOW WHAT'S REAL ANYMORE!!

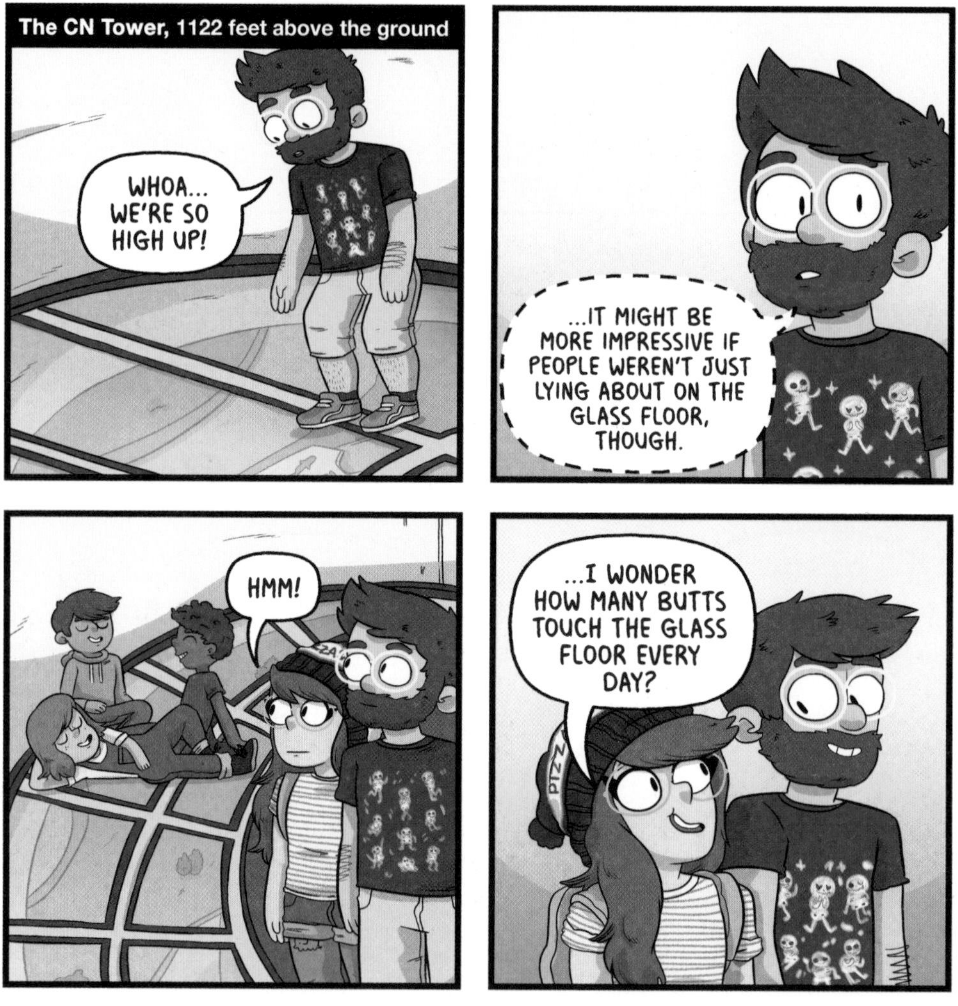
The CN Tower, 1122 feet above the ground
WHOA... WE'RE SO HIGH UP!
...IT MIGHT BE MORE IMPRESSIVE IF PEOPLE WEREN'T JUST LYING ABOUT ON THE GLASS FLOOR, THOUGH.
HMM!
...I WONDER HOW MANY BUTTS TOUCH THE GLASS FLOOR EVERY DAY?

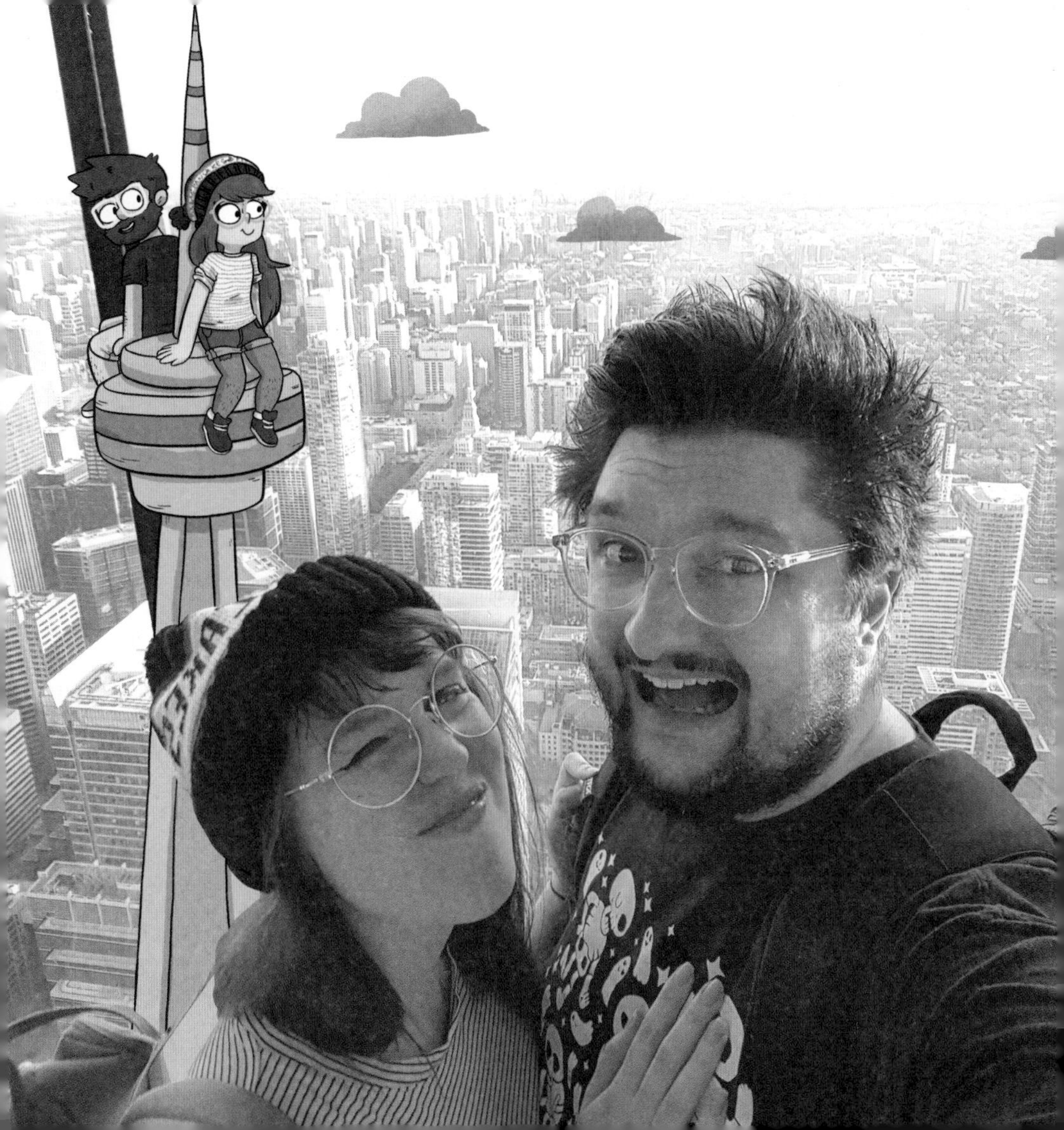

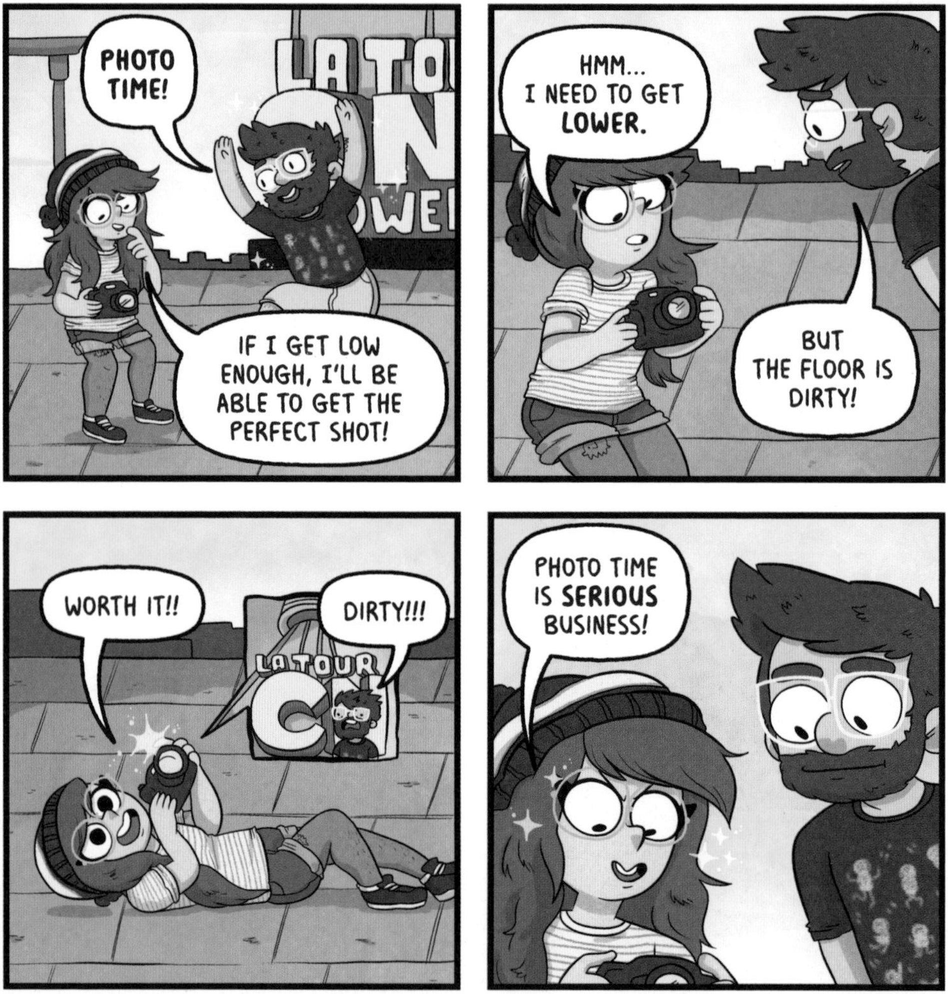
PHOTO TIME!
IF I GET LOW ENOUGH, I'LL BE ABLE TO GET THE PERFECT SHOT!
HMM... I NEED TO GET **LOWER.**
BUT THE FLOOR IS DIRTY!
WORTH IT!!
DIRTY!!!
LATOUR
PHOTO TIME IS **SERIOUS** BUSINESS!

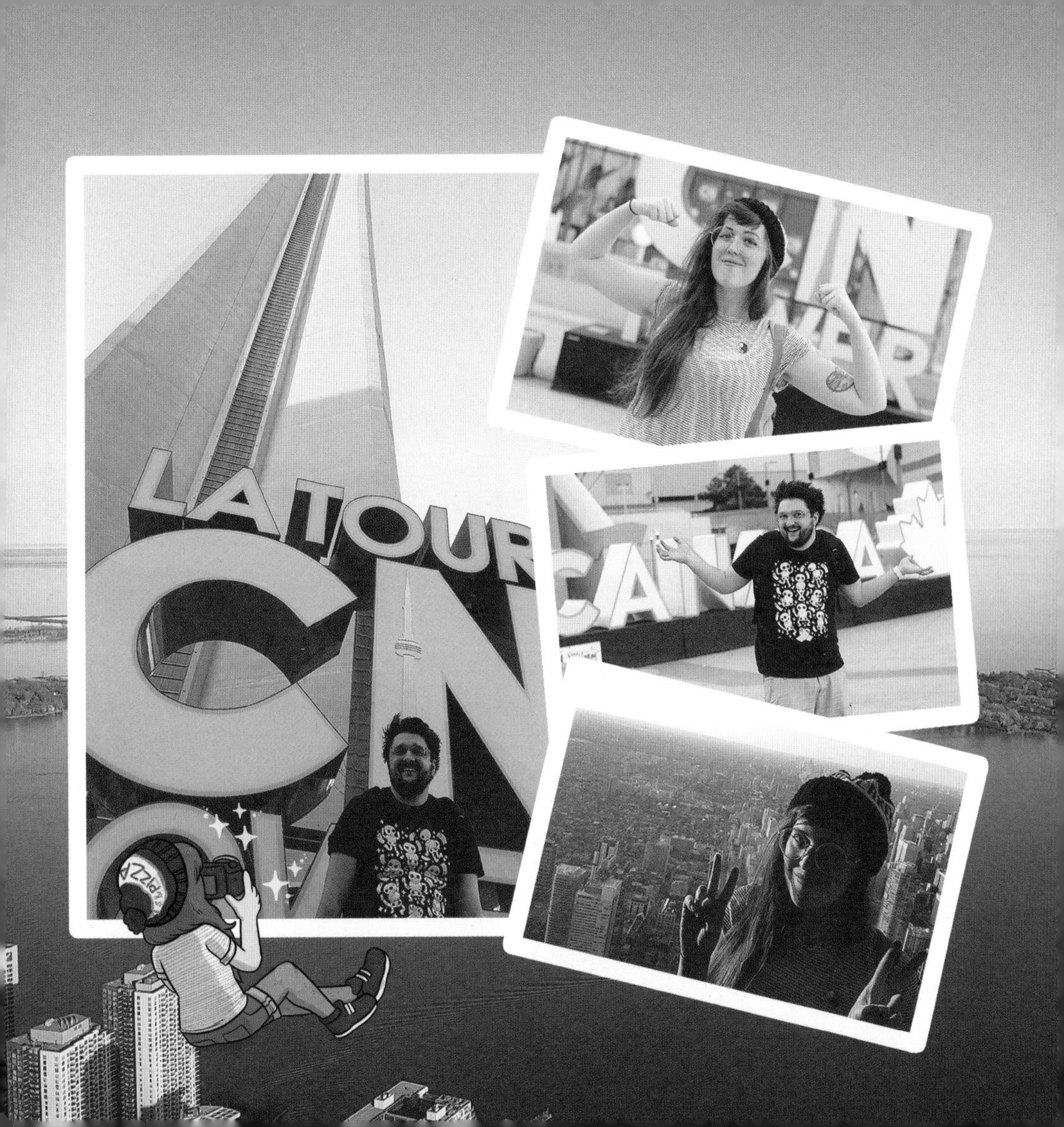
LA TOUR
CN

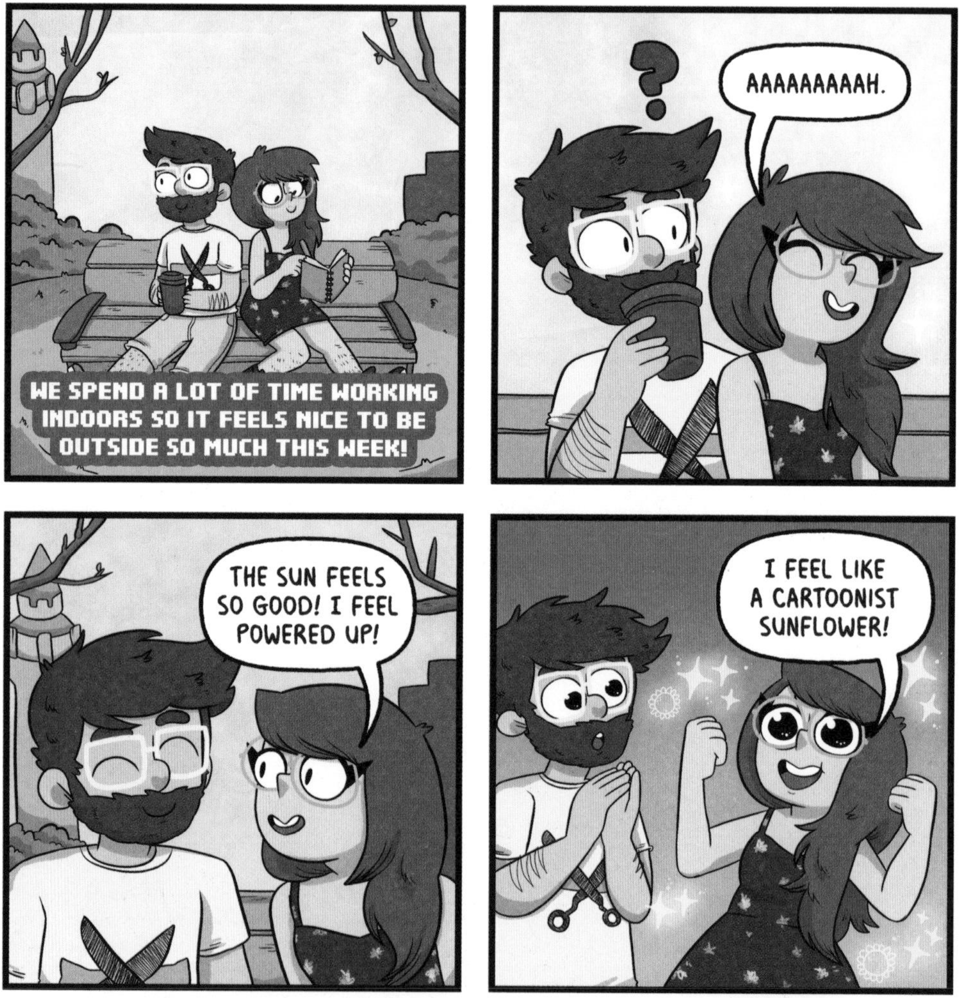
WE SPEND A LOT OF TIME WORKING INDOORS SO IT FEELS NICE TO BE OUTSIDE SO MUCH THIS WEEK!
?
AAAAAAAAAH.
THE SUN FEELS SO GOOD! I FEEL POWERED UP!
I FEEL LIKE A CARTOONIST SUNFLOWER!

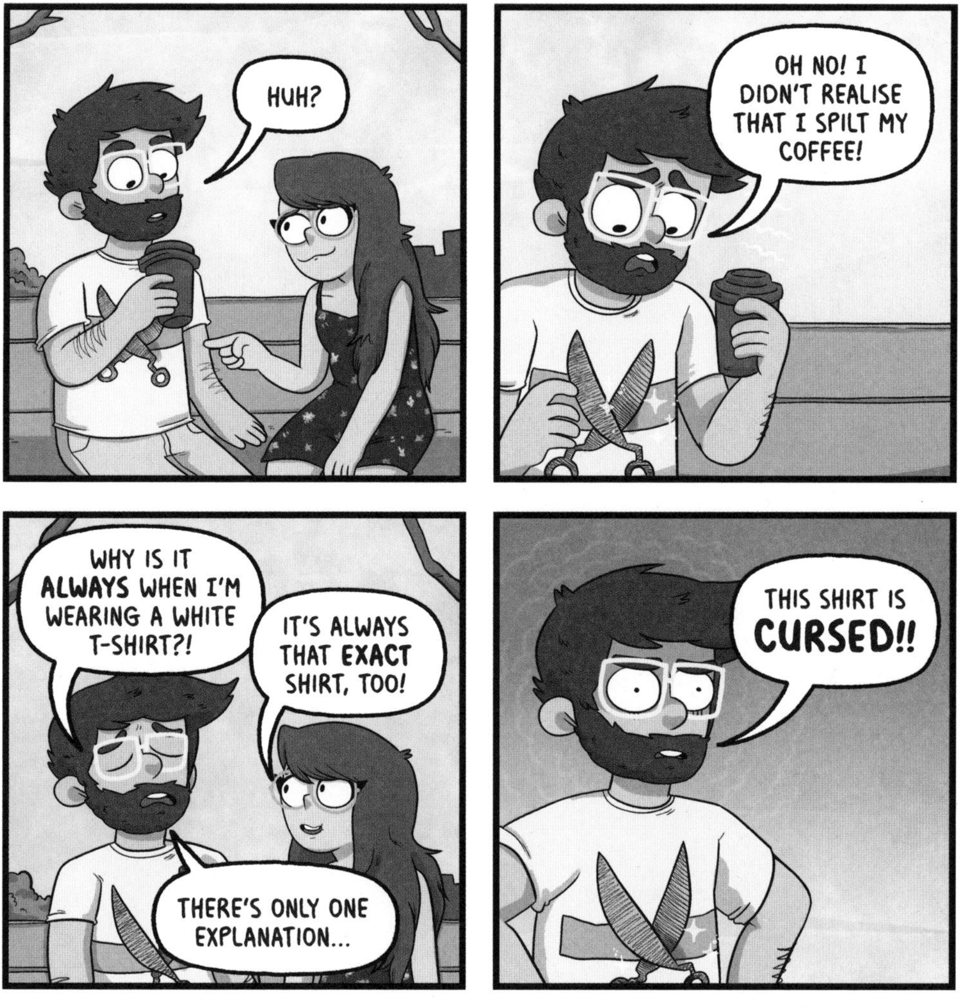
HUH?
OH NO! I DIDN'T REALISE THAT I SPILT MY COFFEE!
WHY IS IT **ALWAYS** WHEN I'M WEARING A WHITE T-SHIRT?!
IT'S ALWAYS THAT **EXACT** SHIRT, TOO!
THERE'S ONLY ONE EXPLANATION...
THIS SHIRT IS **CURSED!!**

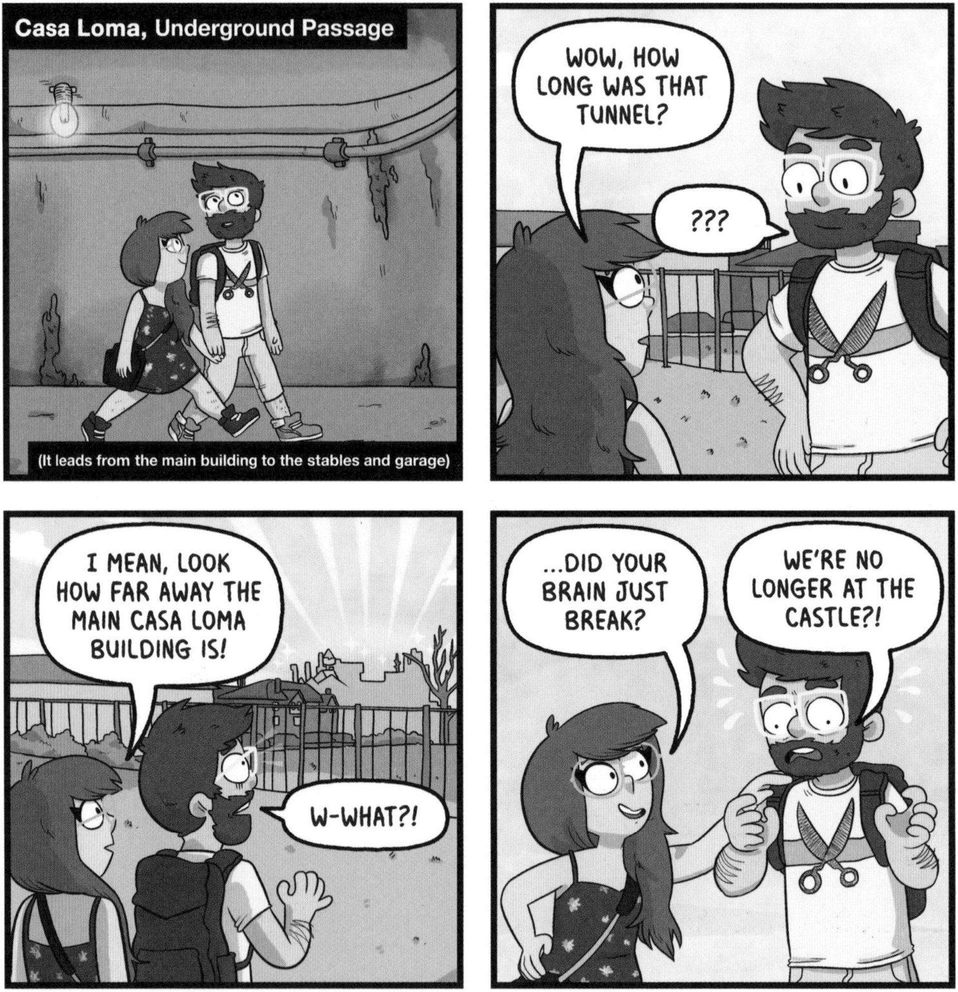
Casa Loma, Underground Passage
(It leads from the main building to the stables and garage)
WOW, HOW LONG WAS THAT TUNNEL?
???
I MEAN, LOOK HOW FAR AWAY THE MAIN CASA LOMA BUILDING IS!
W-WHAT?!
...DID YOUR BRAIN JUST BREAK?
WE'RE NO LONGER AT THE CASTLE?!

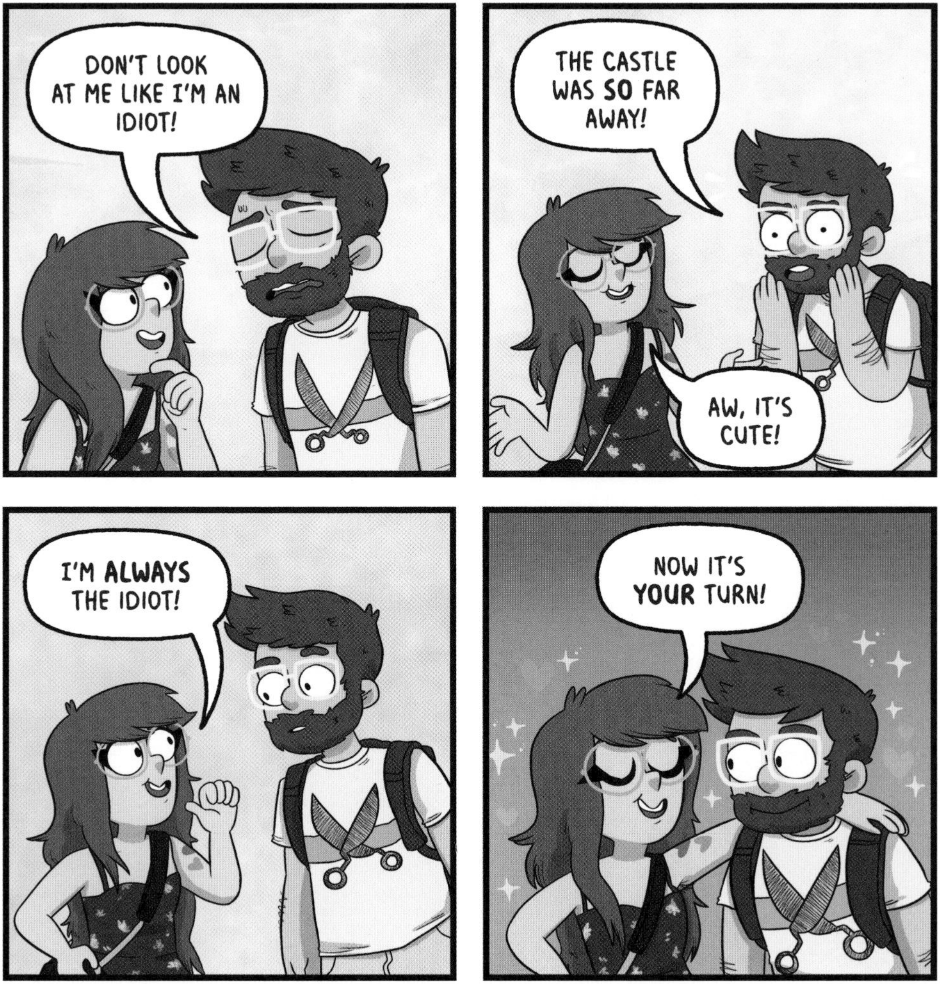
DON'T LOOK AT ME LIKE I'M AN IDIOT!
THE CASTLE WAS **SO** FAR AWAY!
AW, IT'S CUTE!
I'M **ALWAYS** THE IDIOT!
NOW IT'S **YOUR** TURN!

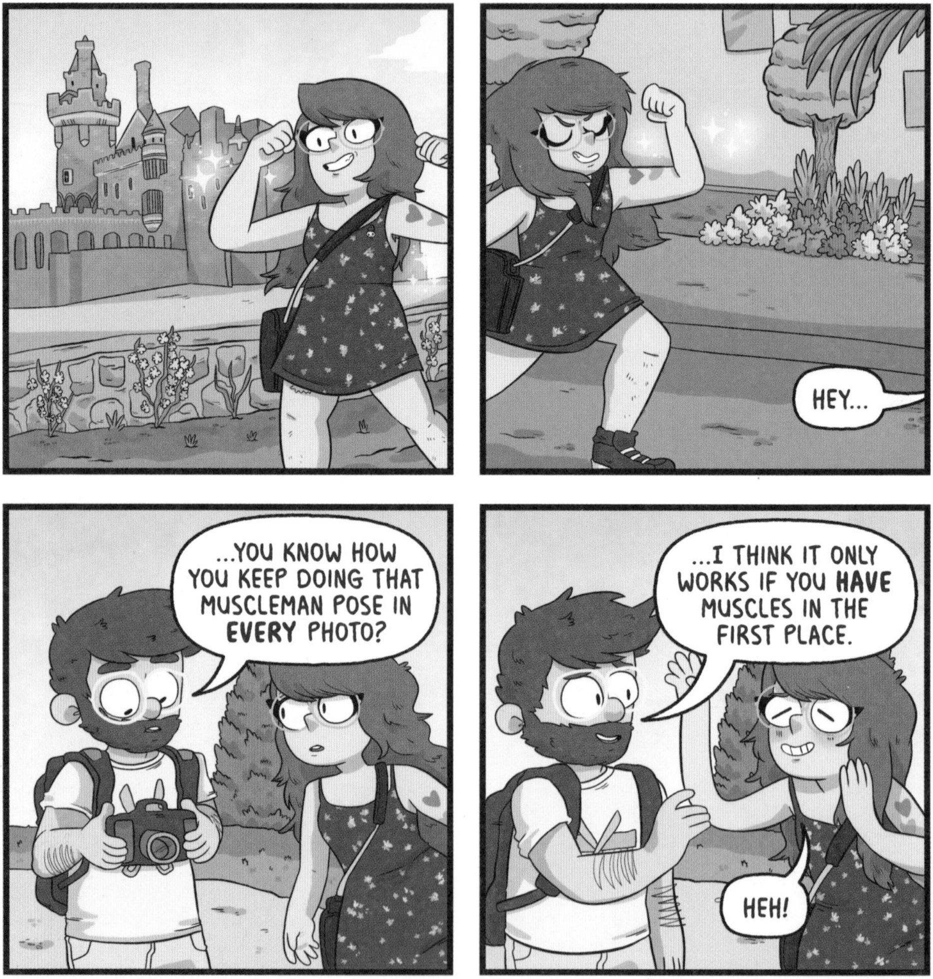
HEY...
...YOU KNOW HOW YOU KEEP DOING THAT MUSCLEMAN POSE IN **EVERY** PHOTO?
...I THINK IT ONLY WORKS IF YOU **HAVE** MUSCLES IN THE FIRST PLACE.
HEH!

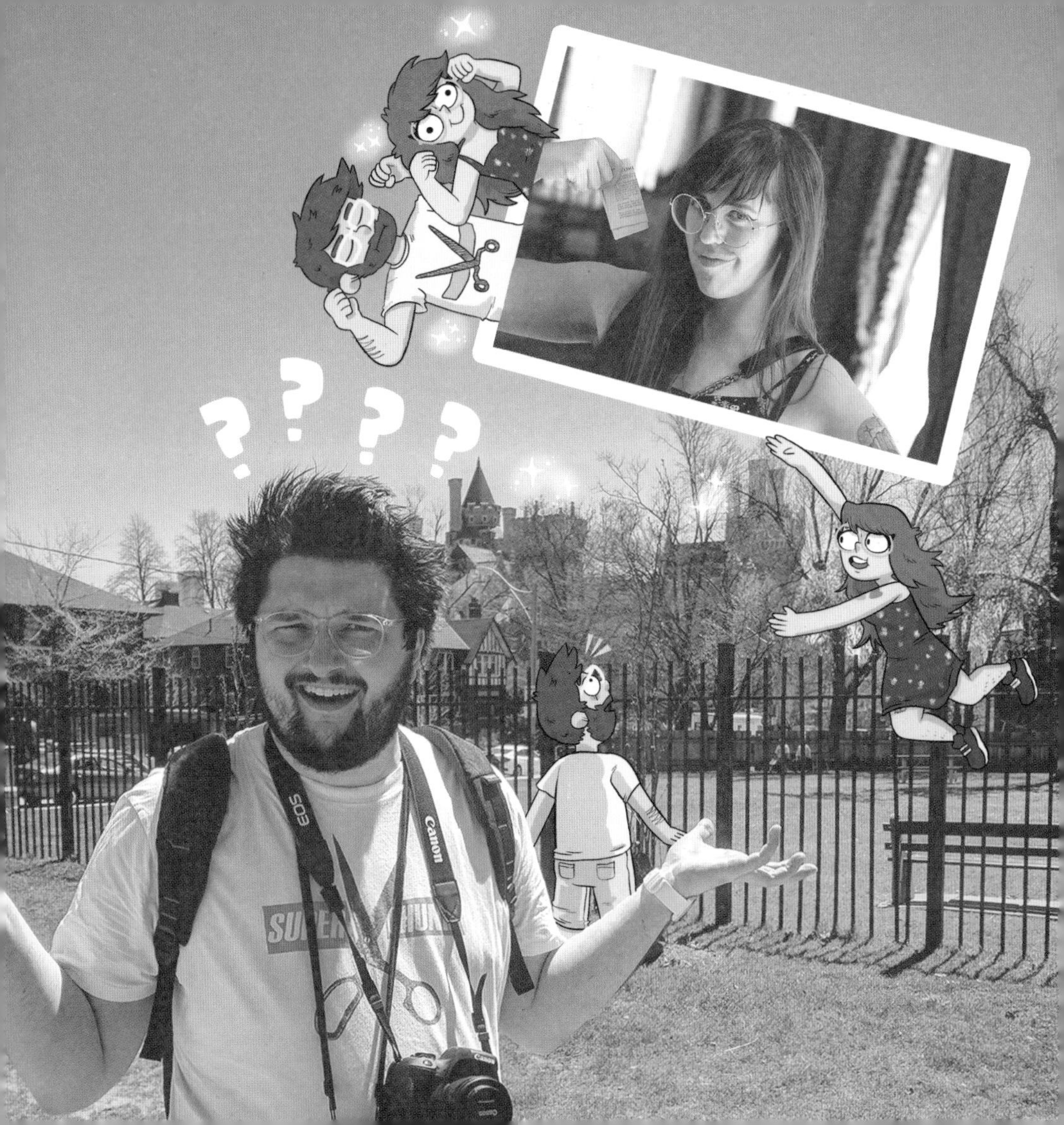
EOS
Canon

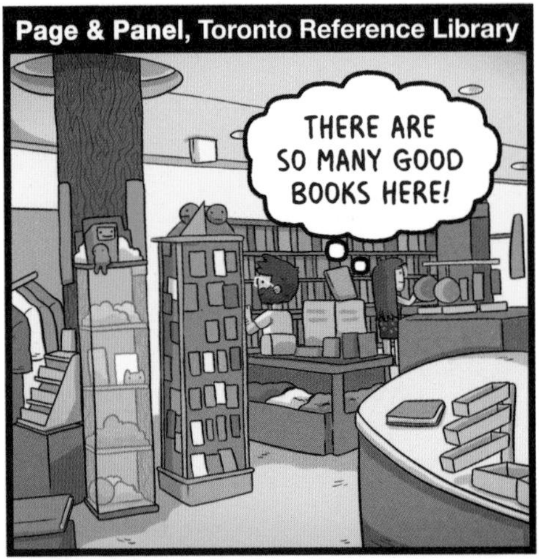
Page & Panel, Toronto Reference Library
THERE ARE SO MANY GOOD BOOKS HERE!

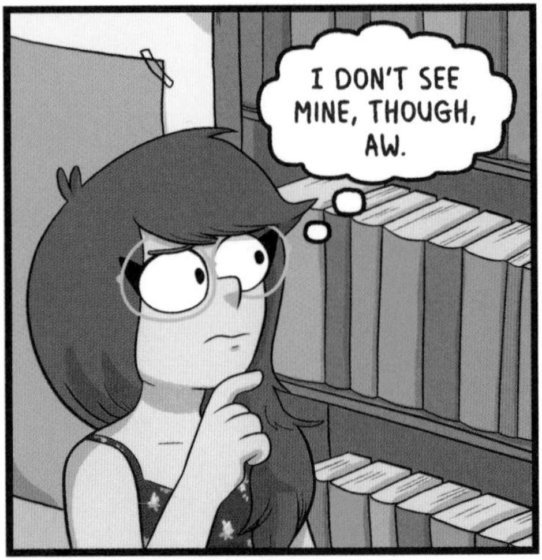
I DON'T SEE MINE, THOUGH, AW.

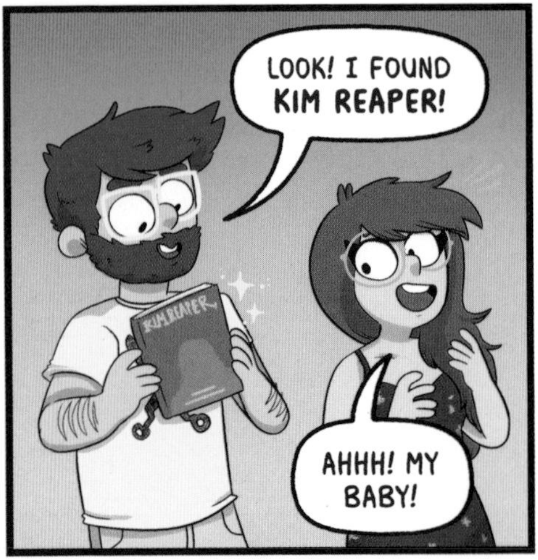
LOOK! I FOUND KIM REAPER!
AHHH! MY BABY!

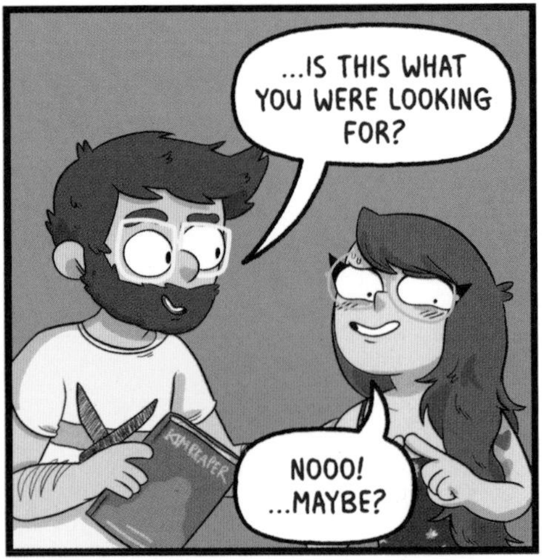
...IS THIS WHAT YOU WERE LOOKING FOR?
NOOO! ...MAYBE?

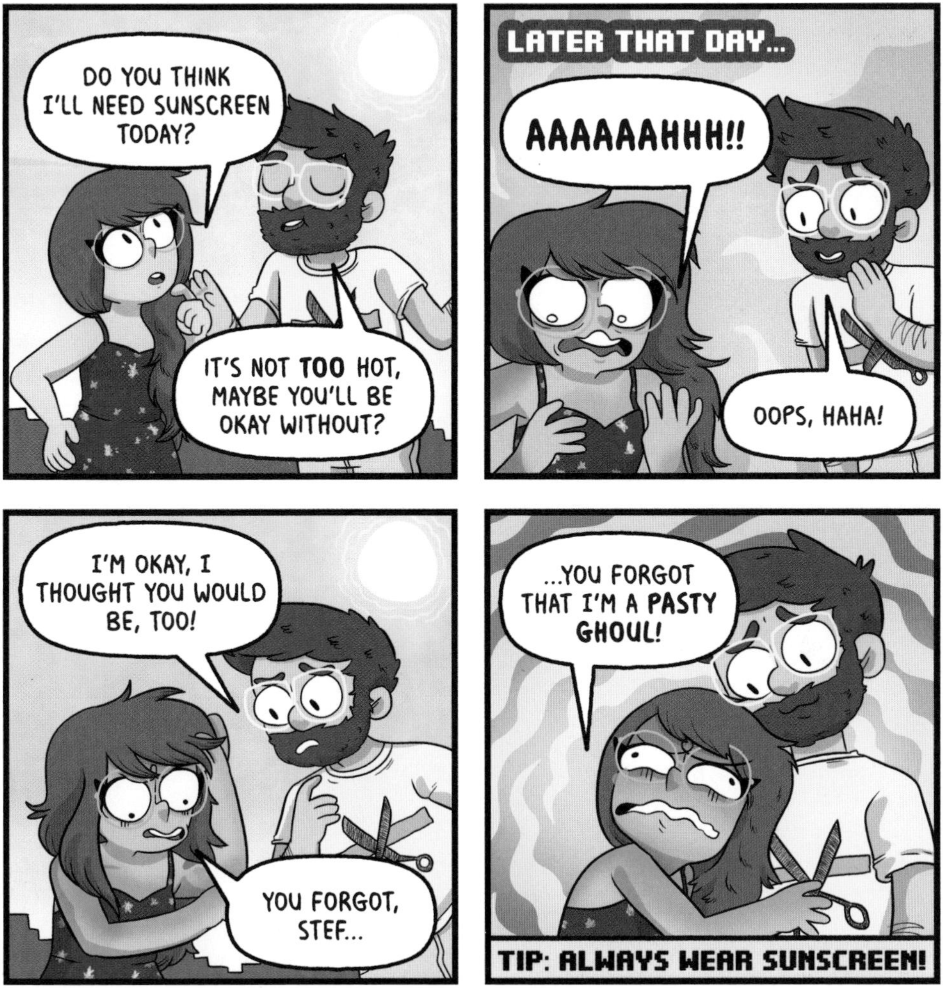
DO YOU THINK I'LL NEED SUNSCREEN TODAY?
IT'S NOT **TOO** HOT, MAYBE YOU'LL BE OKAY WITHOUT?
LATER THAT DAY...
AAAAAAHHH!!
OOPS, HAHA!
I'M OKAY, I THOUGHT YOU WOULD BE, TOO!
YOU FORGOT, STEF...
...YOU FORGOT THAT I'M A **PASTY GHOUL!**
TIP: ALWAYS WEAR SUNSCREEN!

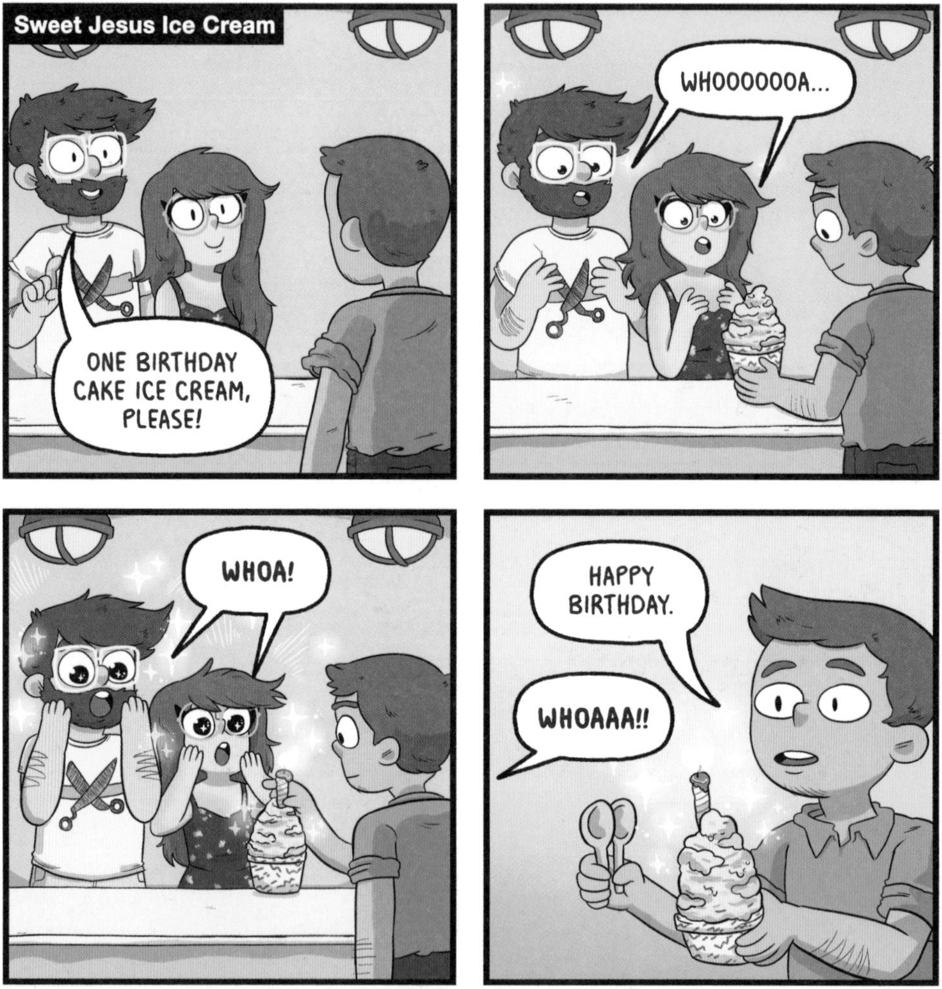
Sweet Jesus Ice Cream
ONE BIRTHDAY CAKE ICE CREAM, PLEASE!
WHOOOOOOA...
WHOA!
HAPPY BIRTHDAY.
WHOAAA!!

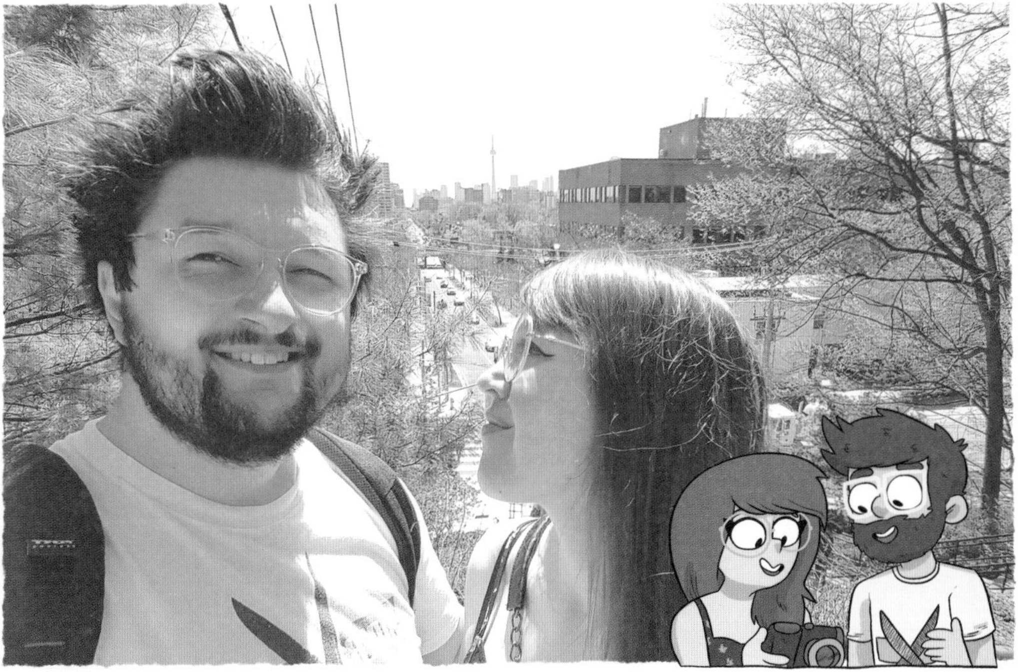

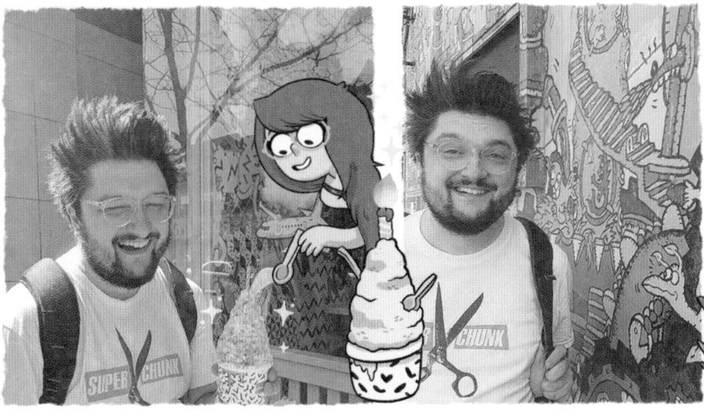
SUPER
CHUNK
CHUNK

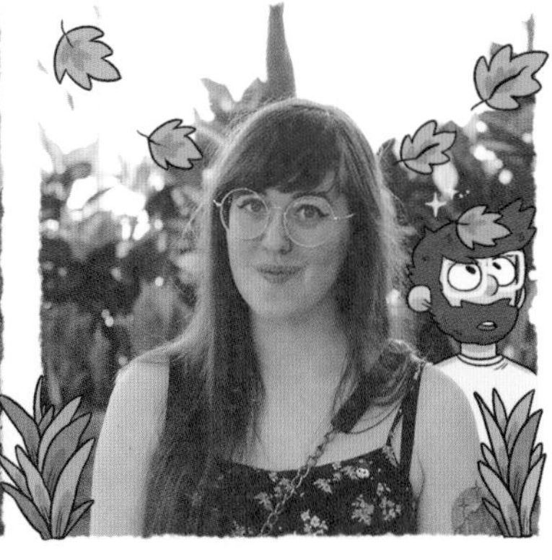

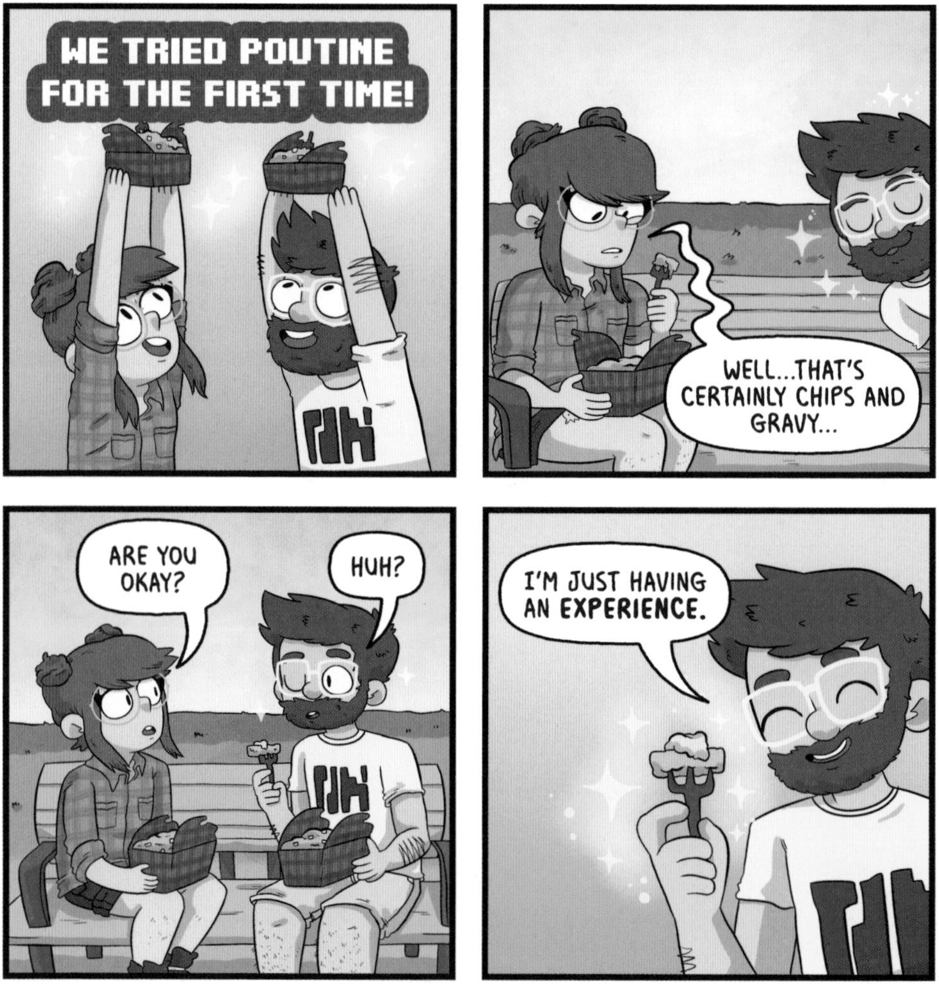
WE TRIED POUTINE FOR THE FIRST TIME!
WELL...THAT'S CERTAINLY CHIPS AND GRAVY...
ARE YOU OKAY?
HUH?
I'M JUST HAVING AN **EXPERIENCE**.

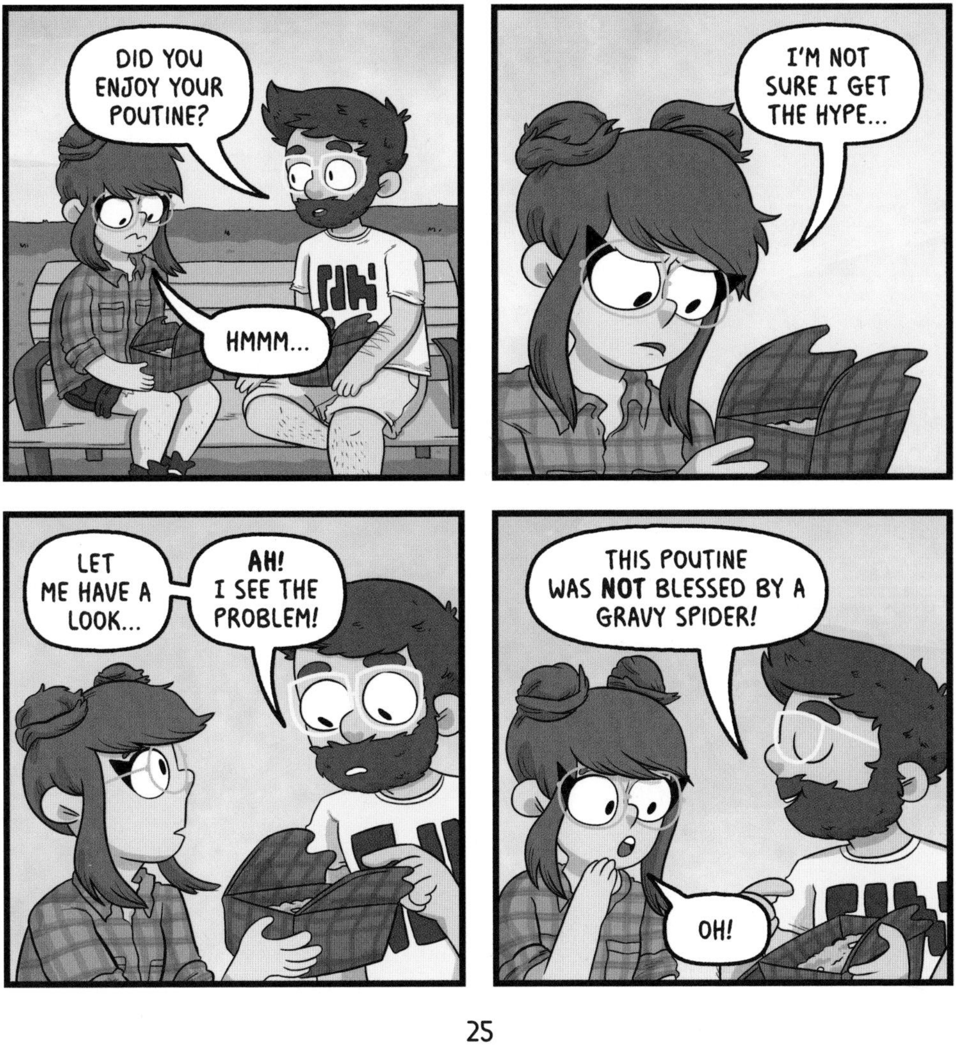
DID YOU ENJOY YOUR POUTINE?
HMMM...
I'M NOT SURE I GET THE HYPE...
LET ME HAVE A LOOK...
AH! I SEE THE PROBLEM!
THIS POUTINE WAS NOT BLESSED BY A GRAVY SPIDER!
OH!

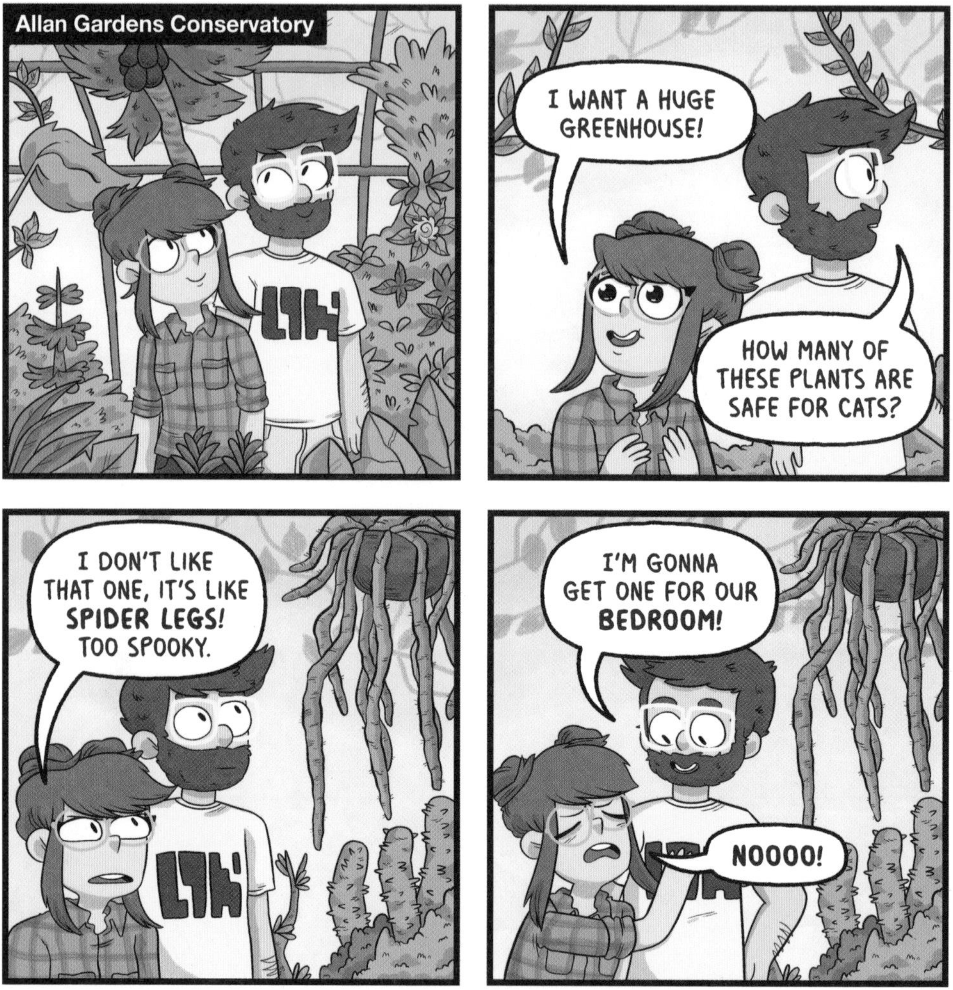
Allan Gardens Conservatory
I WANT A HUGE GREENHOUSE!
HOW MANY OF THESE PLANTS ARE SAFE FOR CATS?
I DON'T LIKE THAT ONE, IT'S LIKE **SPIDER LEGS!** TOO SPOOKY.
I'M GONNA GET ONE FOR OUR **BEDROOM!**
NOOOO!

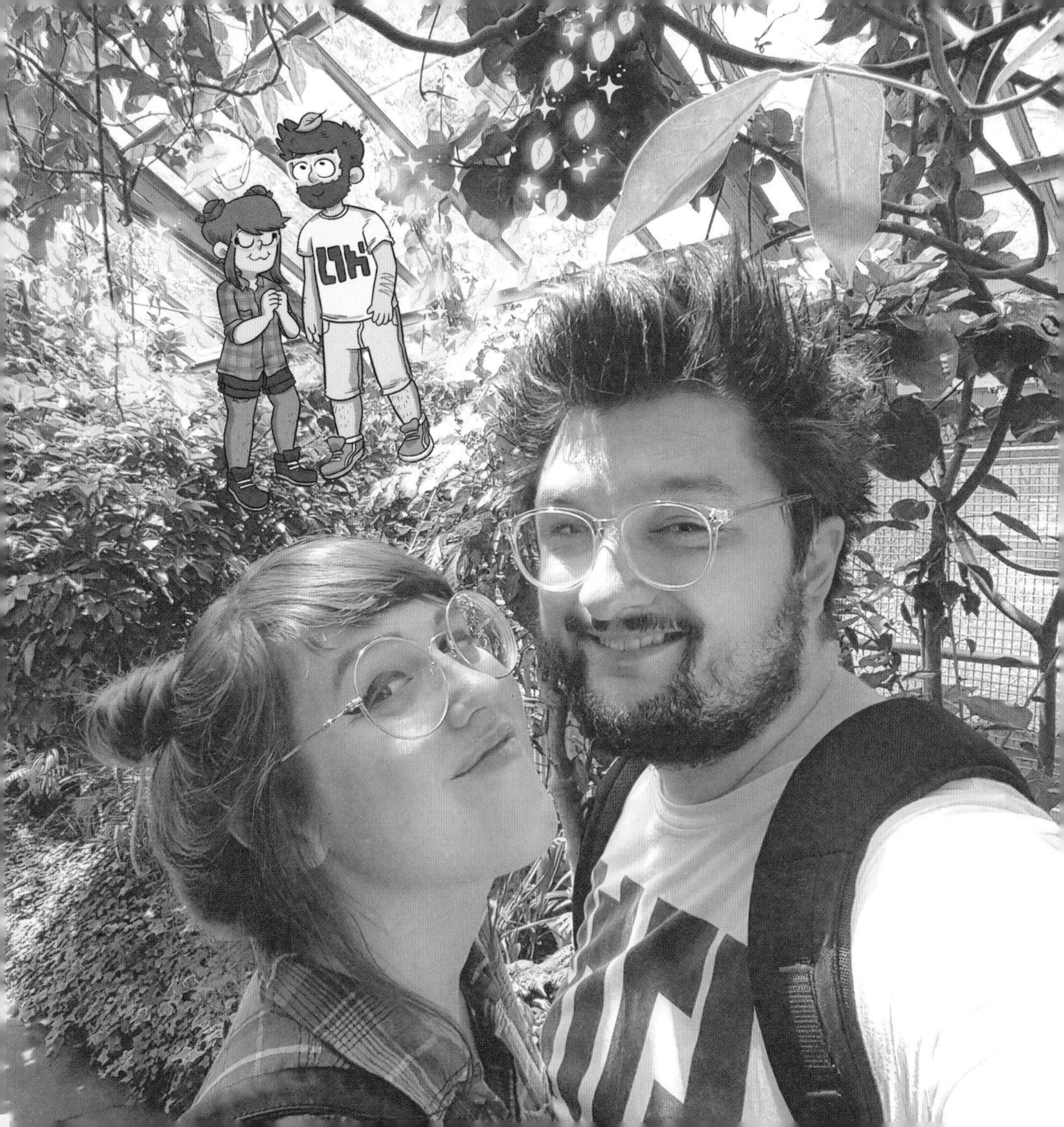

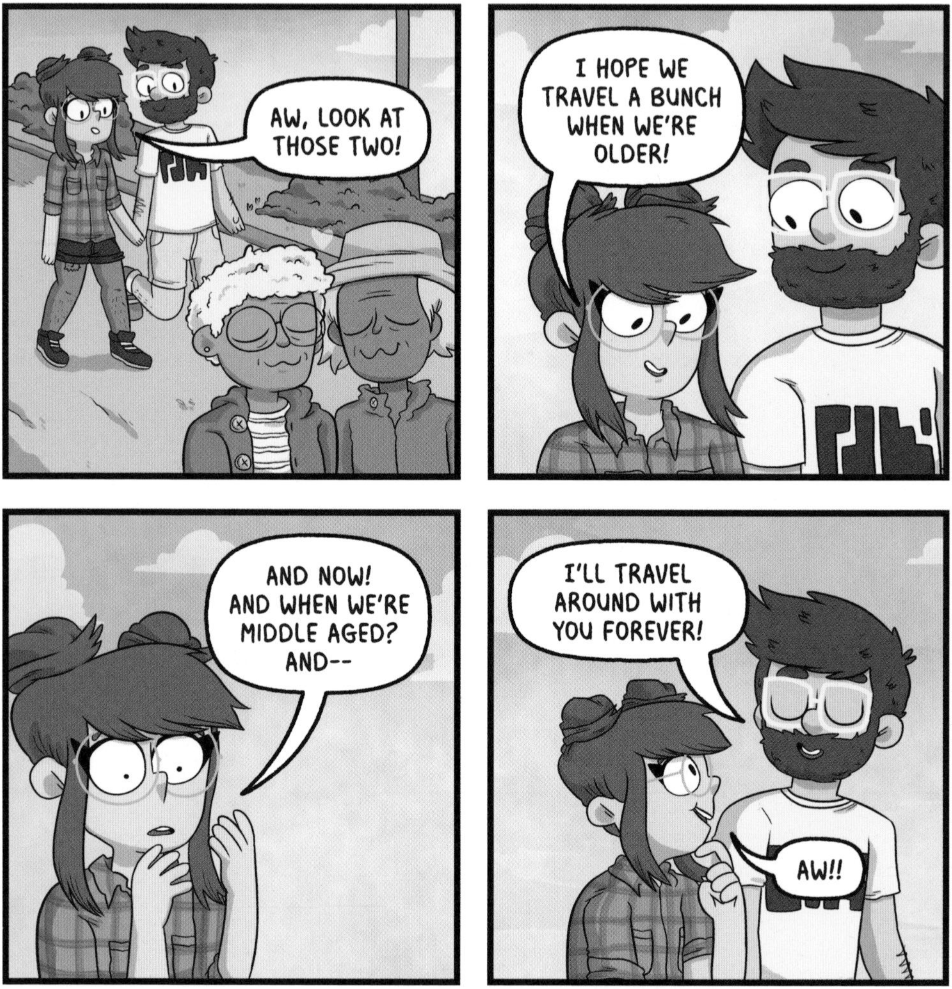
AW, LOOK AT THOSE TWO!
I HOPE WE TRAVEL A BUNCH WHEN WE'RE OLDER!
AND NOW! AND WHEN WE'RE MIDDLE AGED? AND--
I'LL TRAVEL AROUND WITH YOU FOREVER!
AW!!

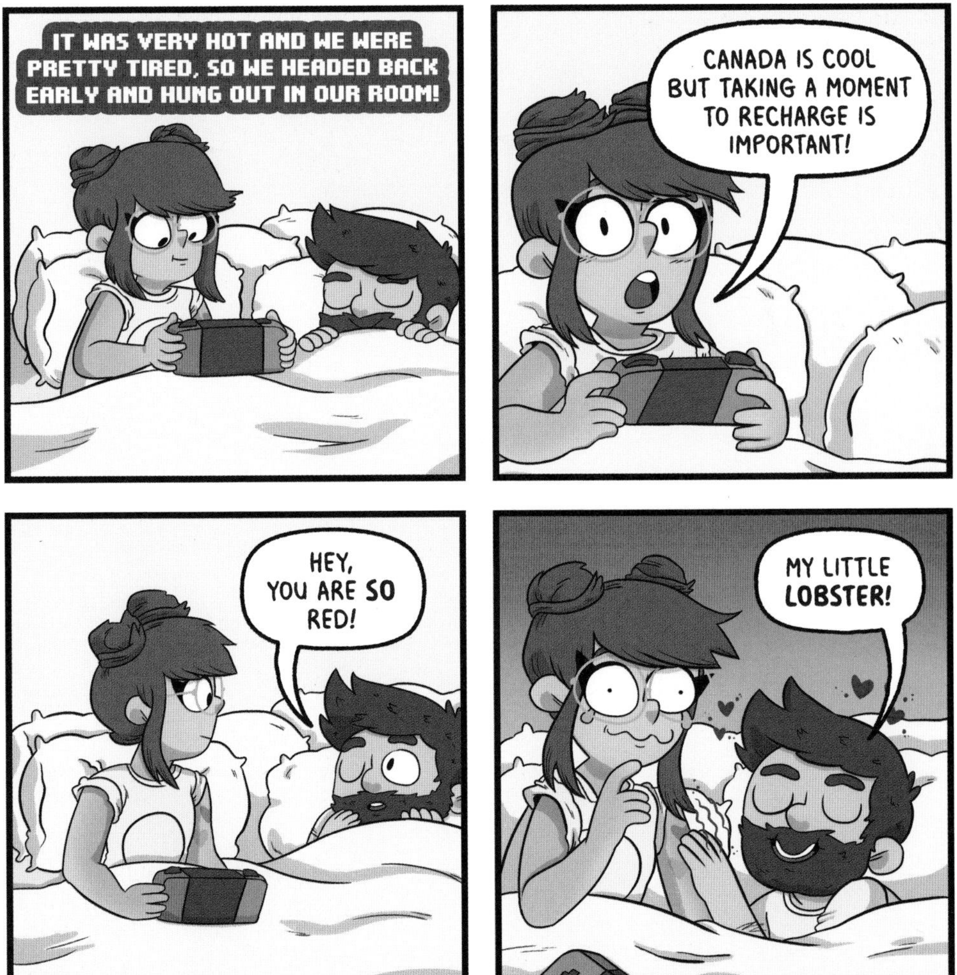
IT WAS VERY HOT AND WE WERE PRETTY TIRED, SO WE HEADED BACK EARLY AND HUNG OUT IN OUR ROOM!
CANADA IS COOL BUT TAKING A MOMENT TO RECHARGE IS IMPORTANT!
HEY, YOU ARE SO RED!
MY LITTLE LOBSTER!

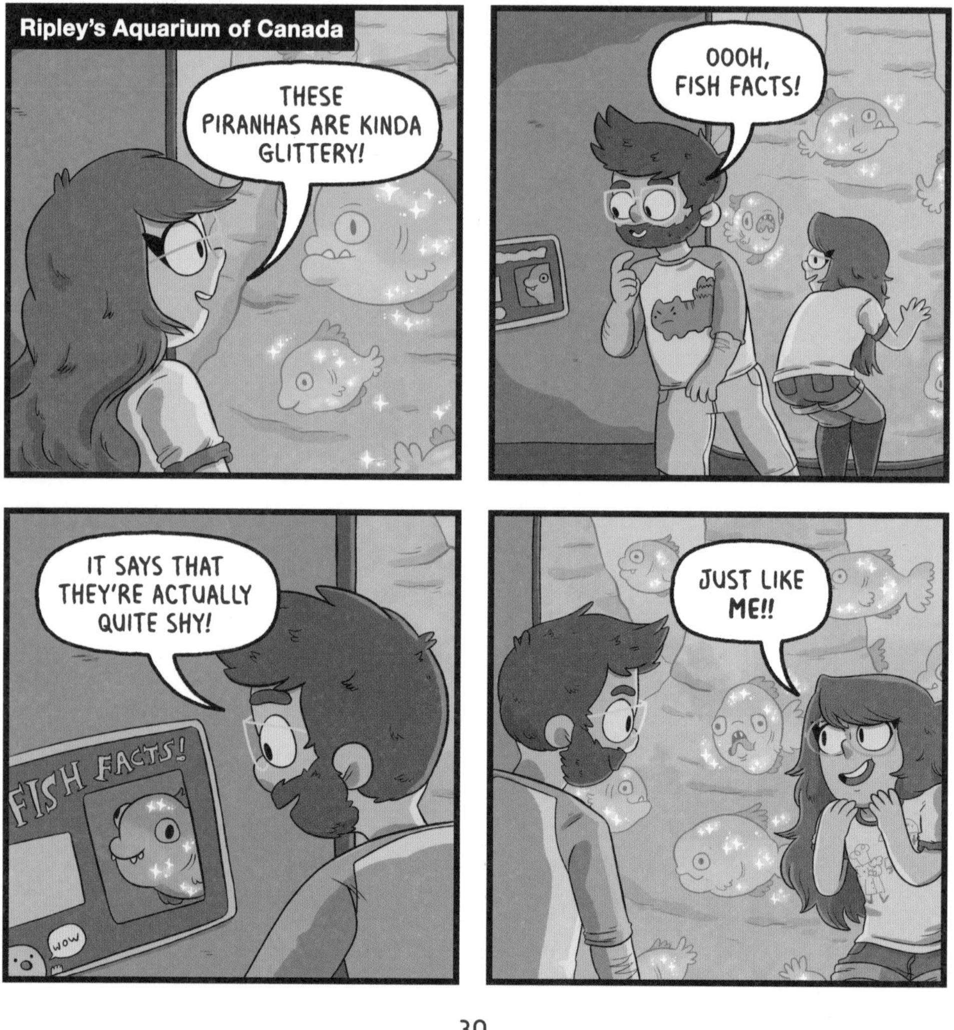
Ripley's Aquarium of Canada
THESE PIRANHAS ARE KINDA GLITTERY!
OOOH, FISH FACTS!
IT SAYS THAT THEY'RE ACTUALLY QUITE SHY!
FISH FACTS!
WOW
JUST LIKE ME!!

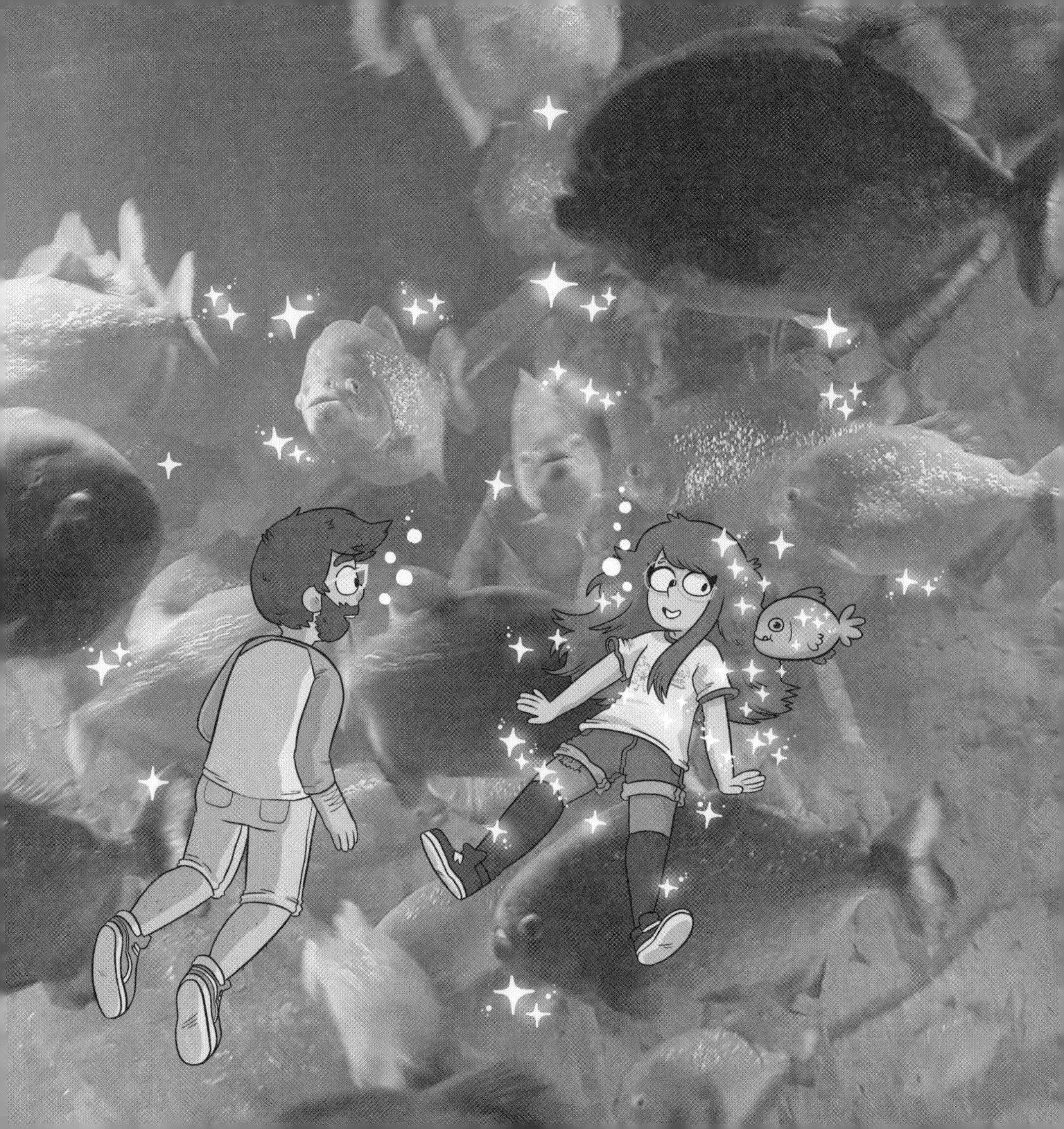

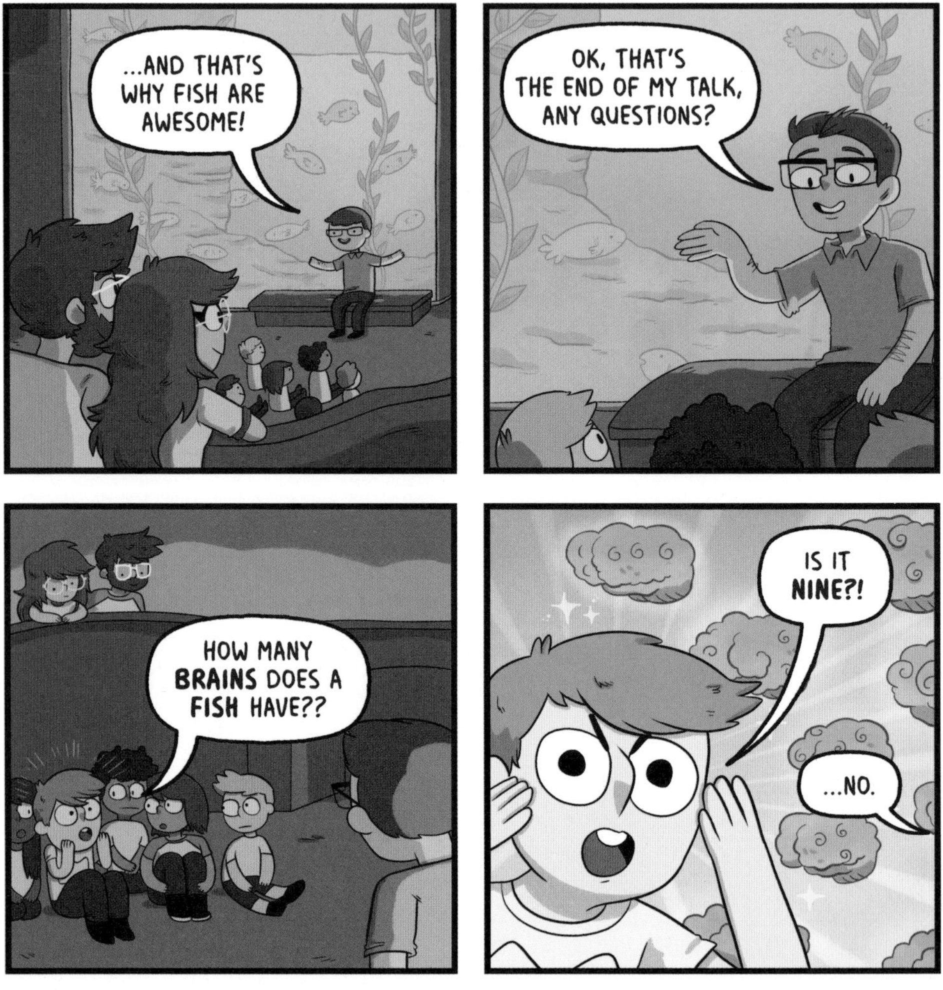
...AND THAT'S WHY FISH ARE AWESOME!
OK, THAT'S THE END OF MY TALK, ANY QUESTIONS?
HOW MANY **BRAINS** DOES A **FISH** HAVE??
IS IT **NINE?!**
...NO.

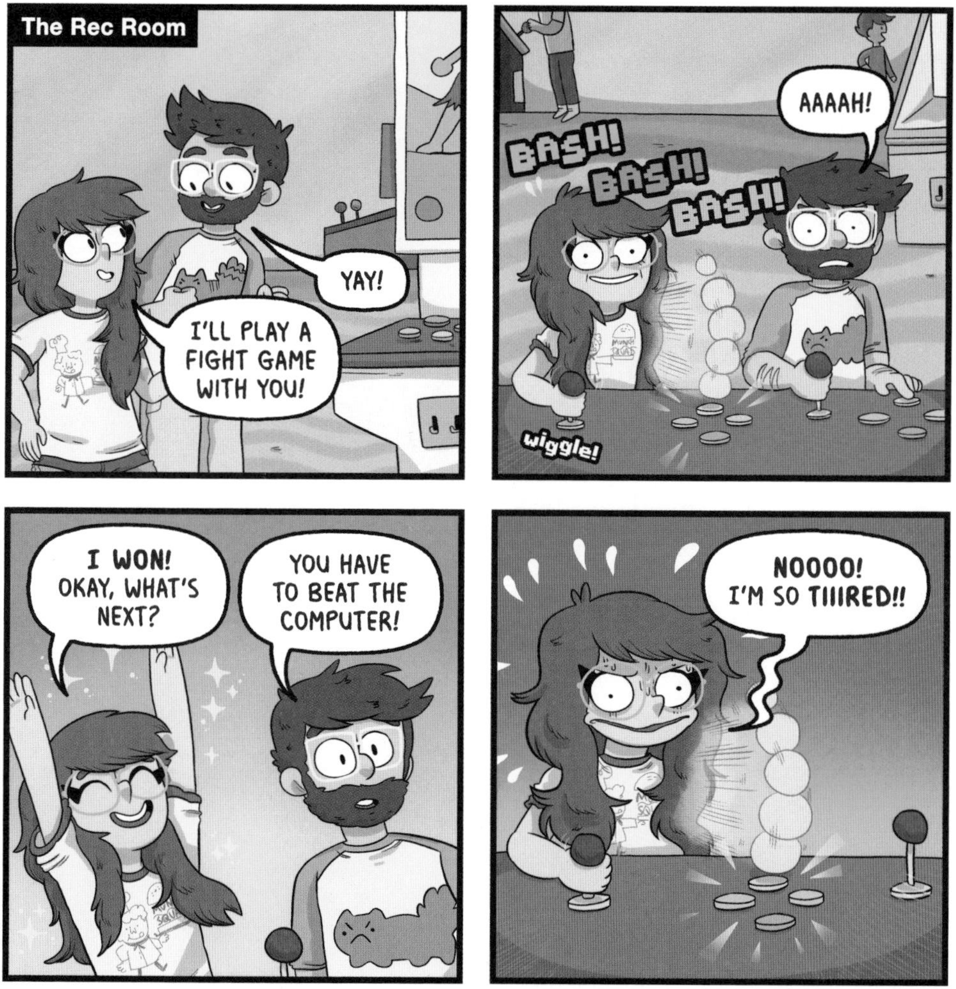
The Rec Room
I'LL PLAY A FIGHT GAME WITH YOU!
YAY!
BASH! BASH! BASH!
AAAAH!
wiggle!
I WON! OKAY, WHAT'S NEXT?
YOU HAVE TO BEAT THE COMPUTER!
NOOOO! I'M SO TIIIRED!!

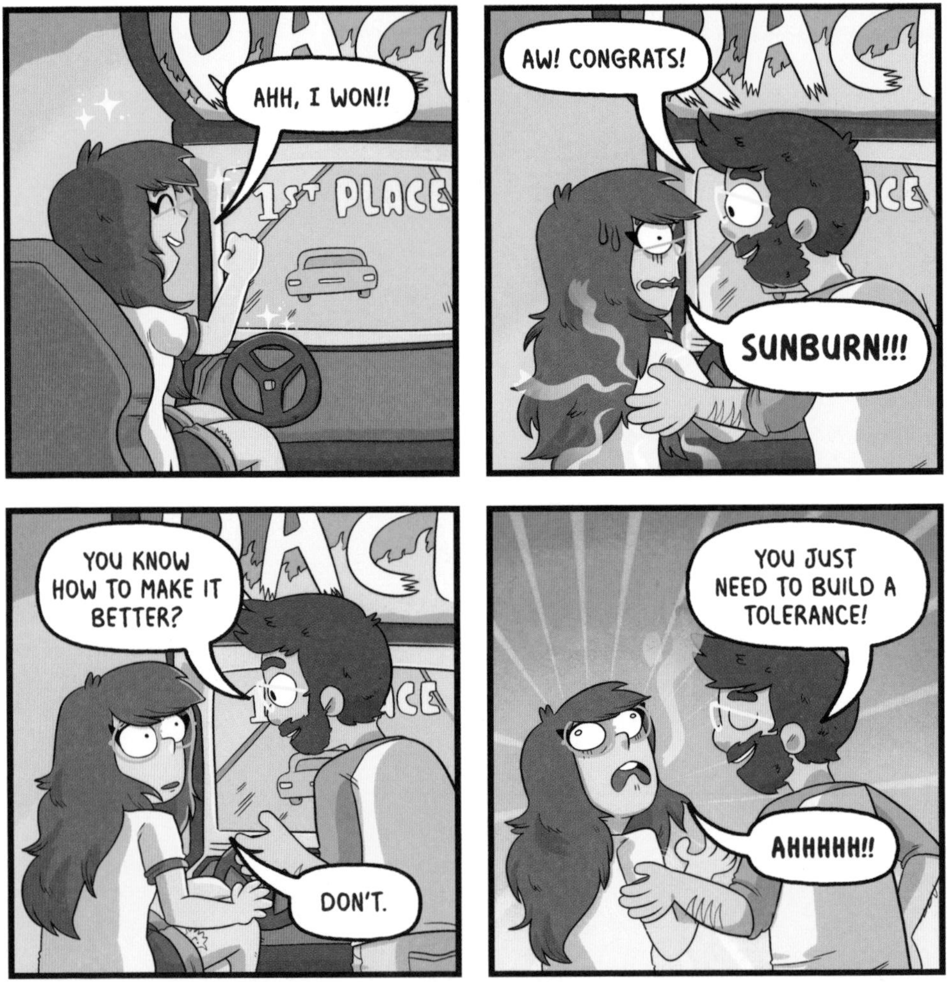
AHH, I WON!!
1ST PLACE
AW! CONGRATS!
SUNBURN!!!
YOU KNOW HOW TO MAKE IT BETTER?
DON'T.
YOU JUST NEED TO BUILD A TOLERANCE!
AHHHHH!!

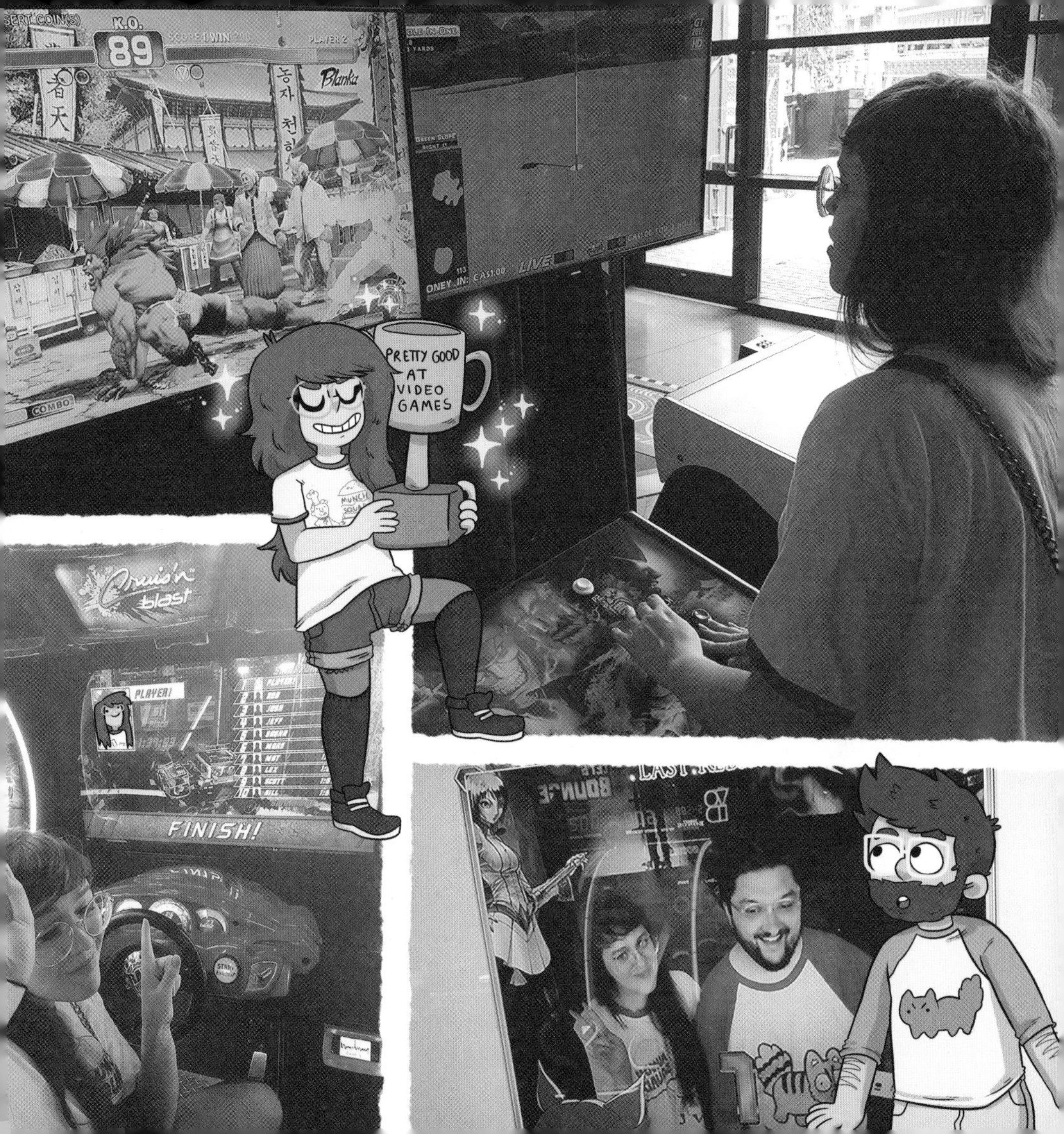
K.O.
89
PLAYER 2
Blanka
COMBO
PRETTY GOOD AT VIDEO GAMES
MUNCH SQUAD
Cruis'n blast
PLAYER1
FINISH!
LIVE
BOUNCE

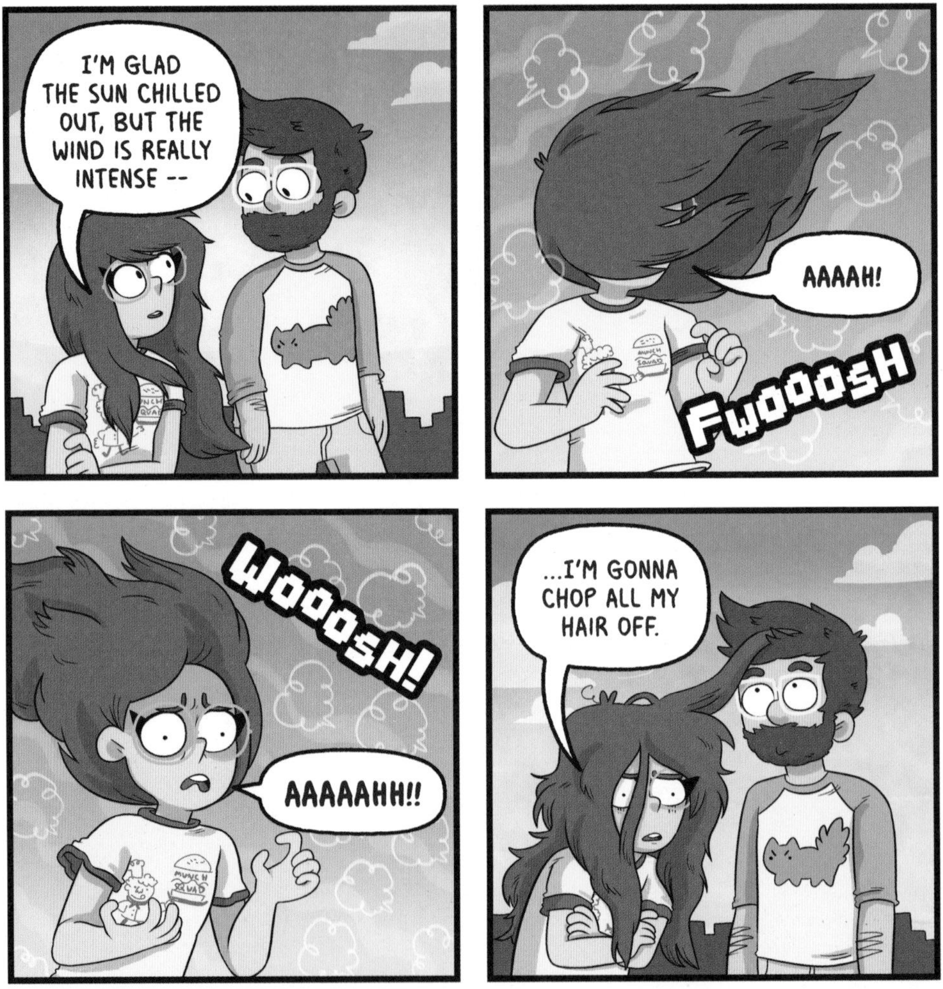

I'M GLAD THE SUN CHILLED OUT, BUT THE WIND IS REALLY INTENSE --
AAAAH!
FWOOOOSH
WOOOOSH!
AAAAAHH!!
...I'M GONNA CHOP ALL MY HAIR OFF.

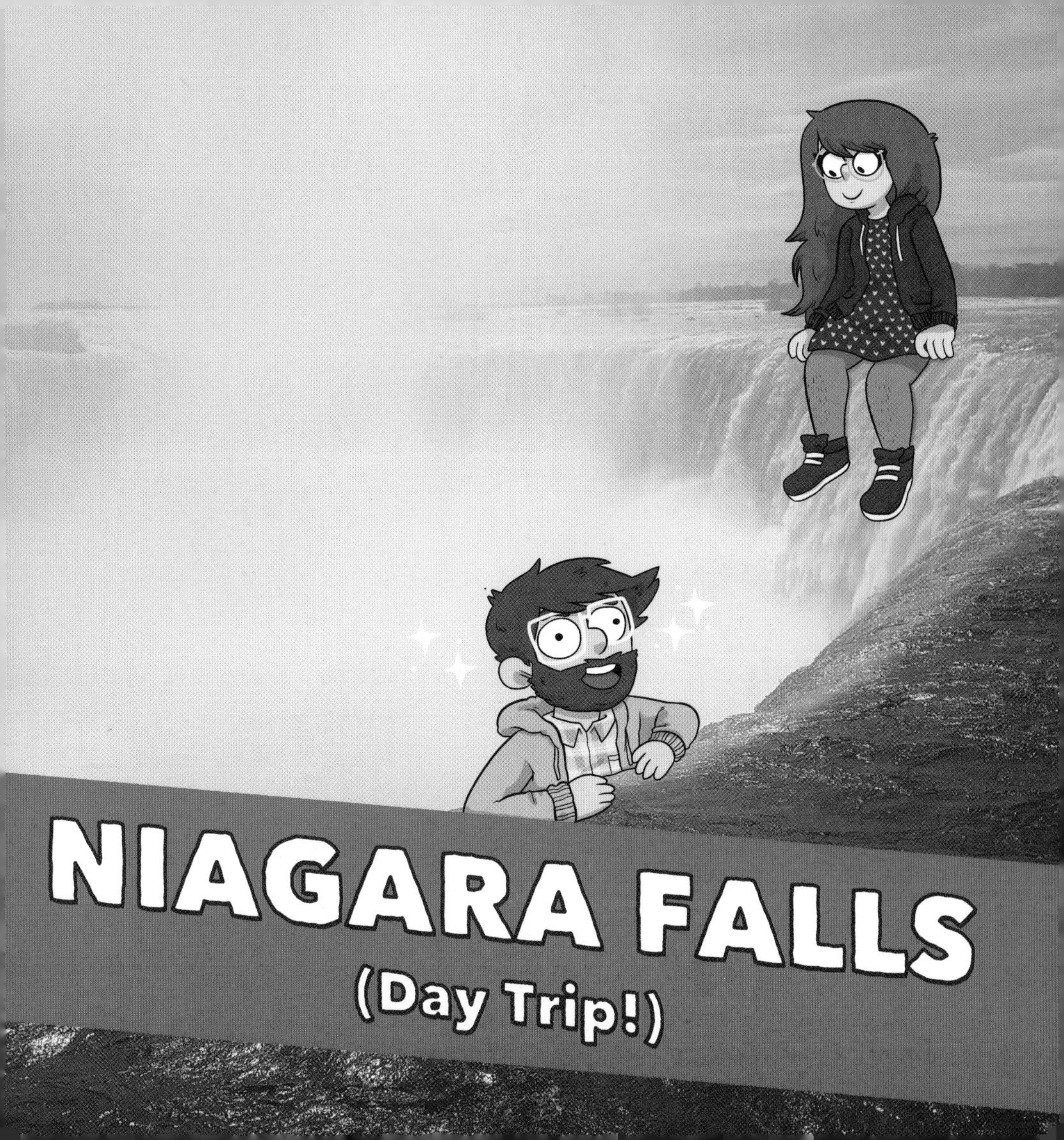
NIAGARA FALLS
(Day Trip!)

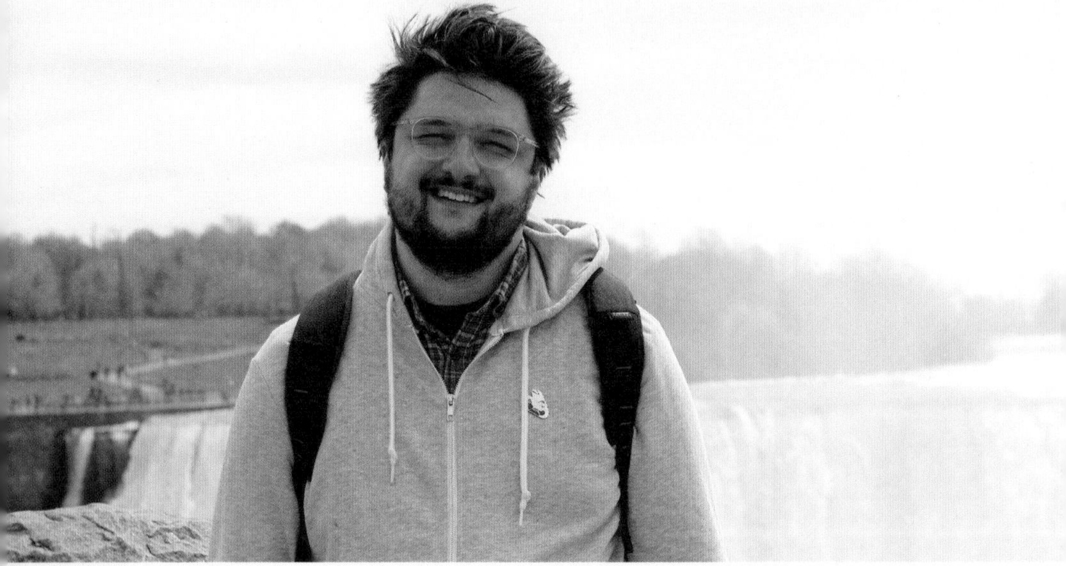

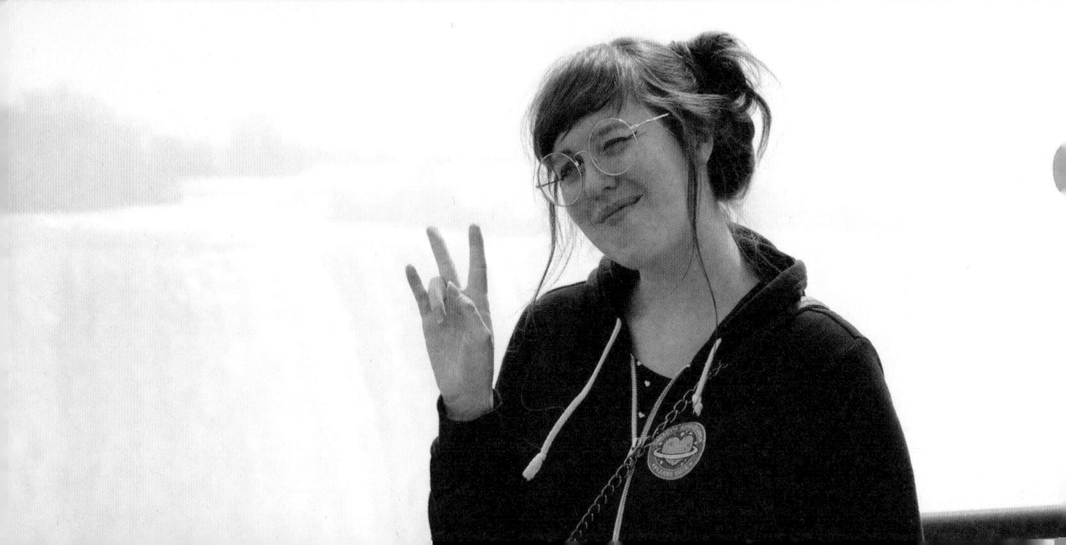

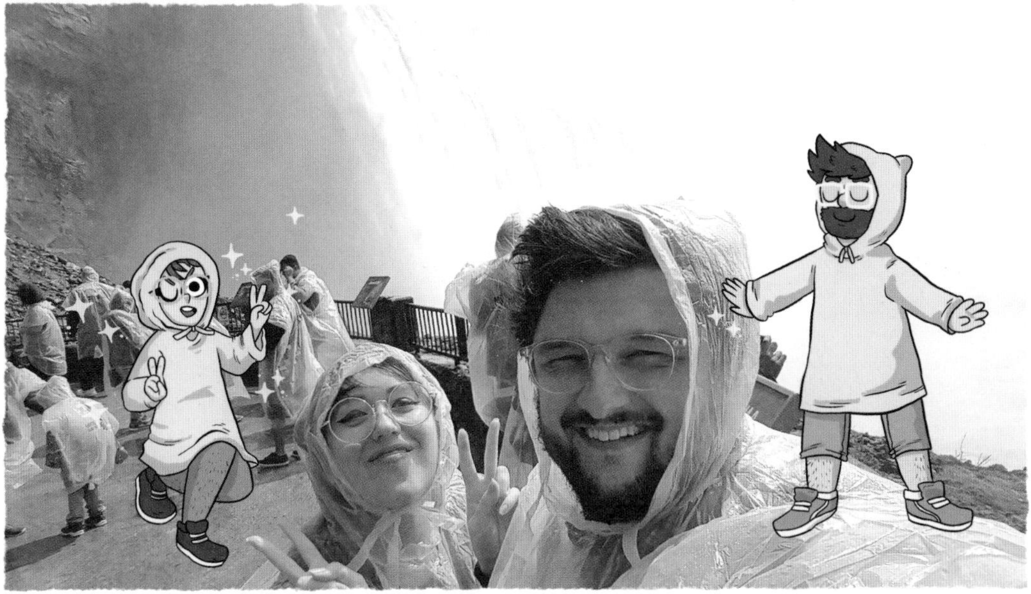

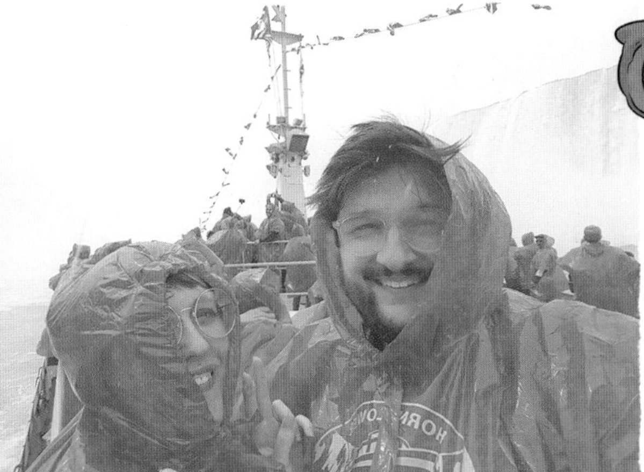

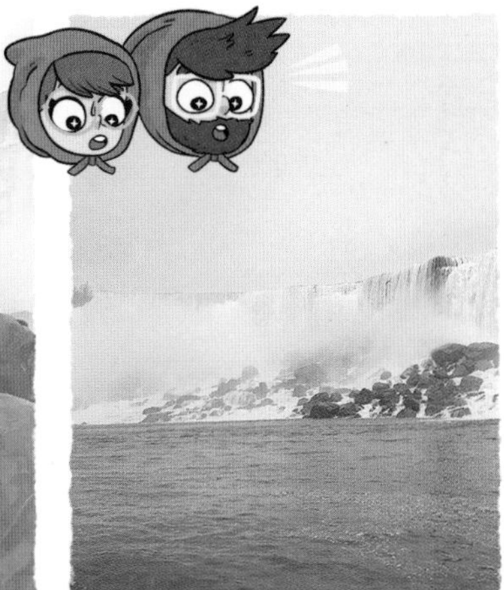

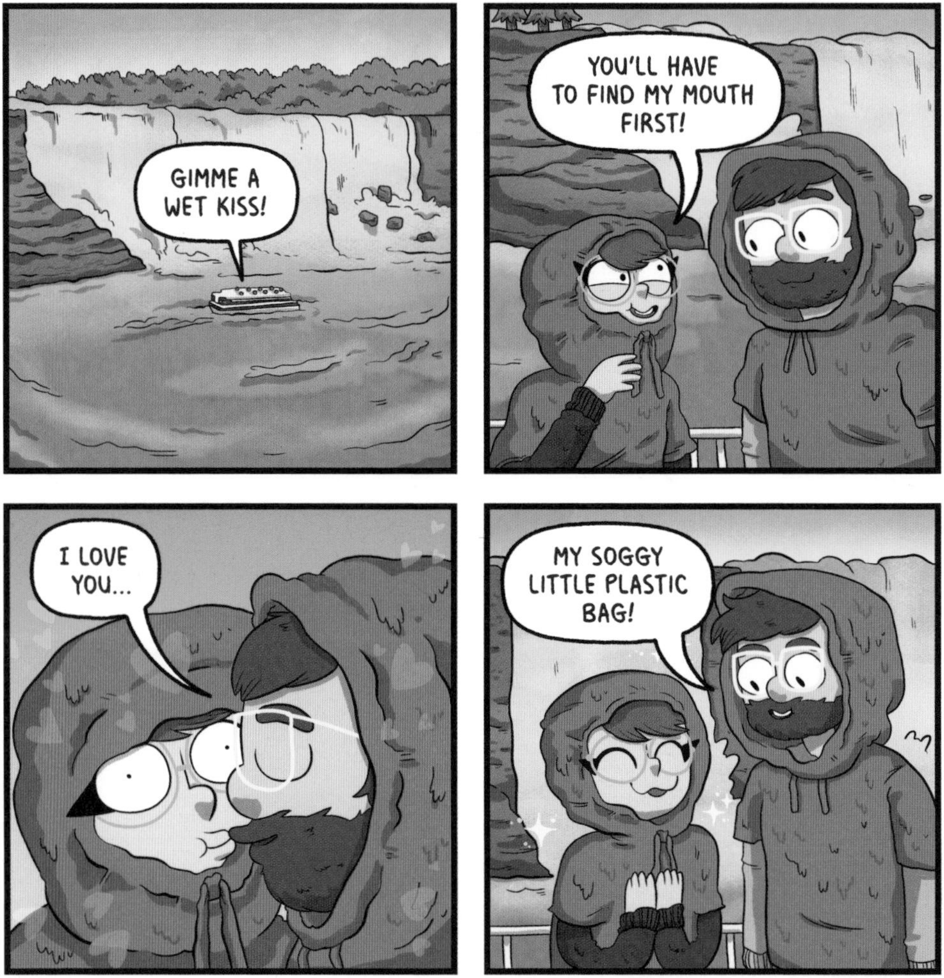
GIMME A WET KISS!
YOU'LL HAVE TO FIND MY MOUTH FIRST!
I LOVE YOU...
MY SOGGY LITTLE PLASTIC BAG!

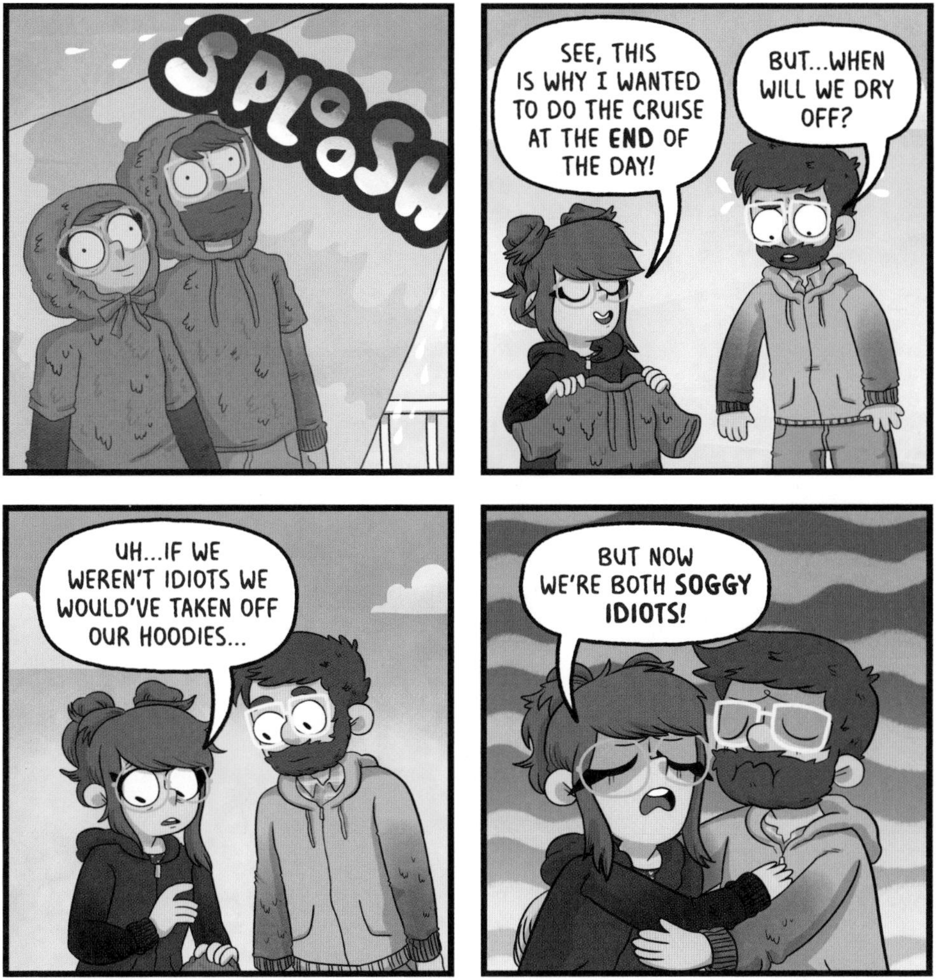
SPLOSH
SEE, THIS IS WHY I WANTED TO DO THE CRUISE AT THE **END** OF THE DAY!
BUT...WHEN WILL WE DRY OFF?
UH...IF WE WEREN'T IDIOTS WE WOULD'VE TAKEN OFF OUR HOODIES...
BUT NOW WE'RE BOTH **SOGGY IDIOTS**!

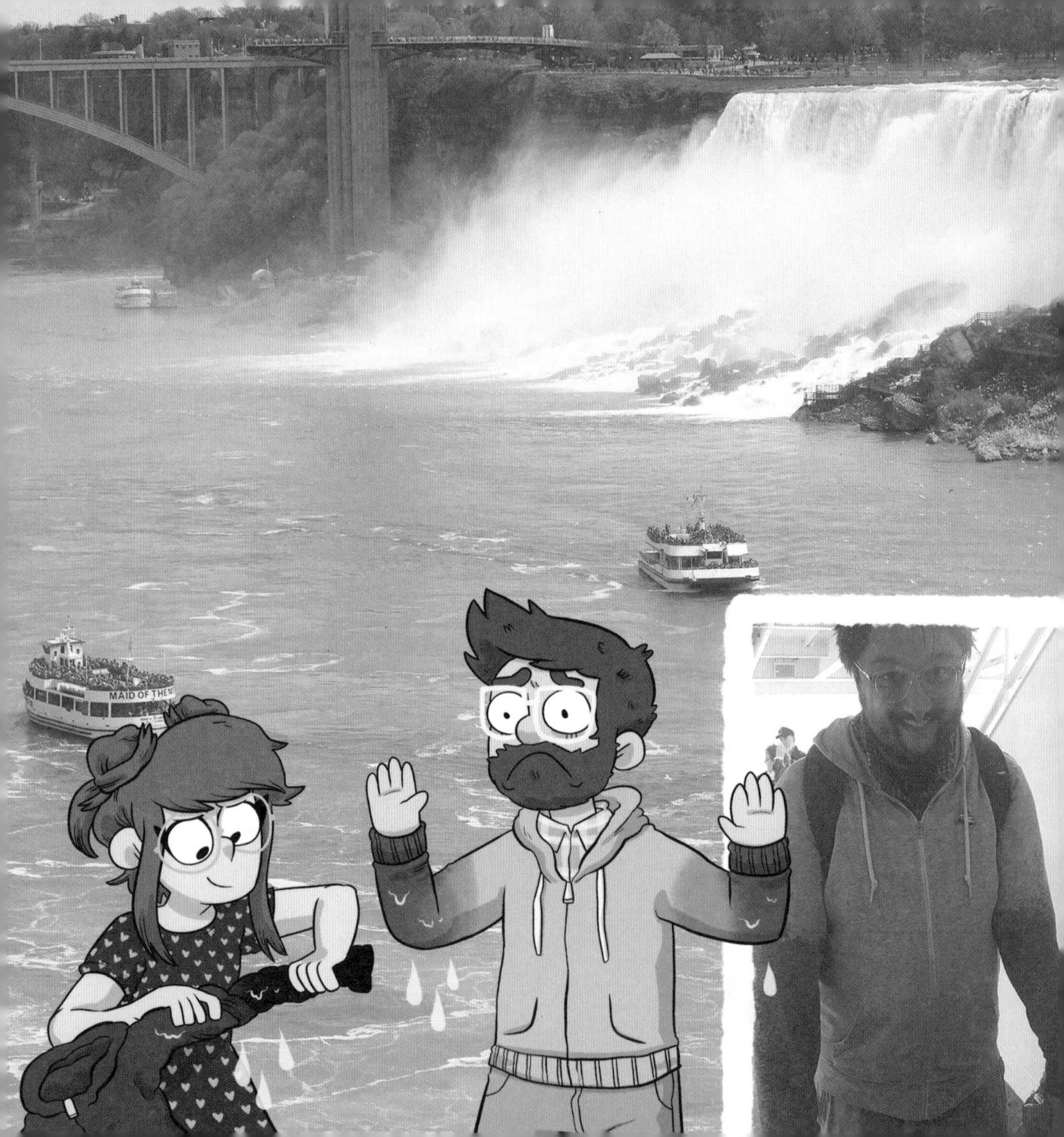
MAID OF THE

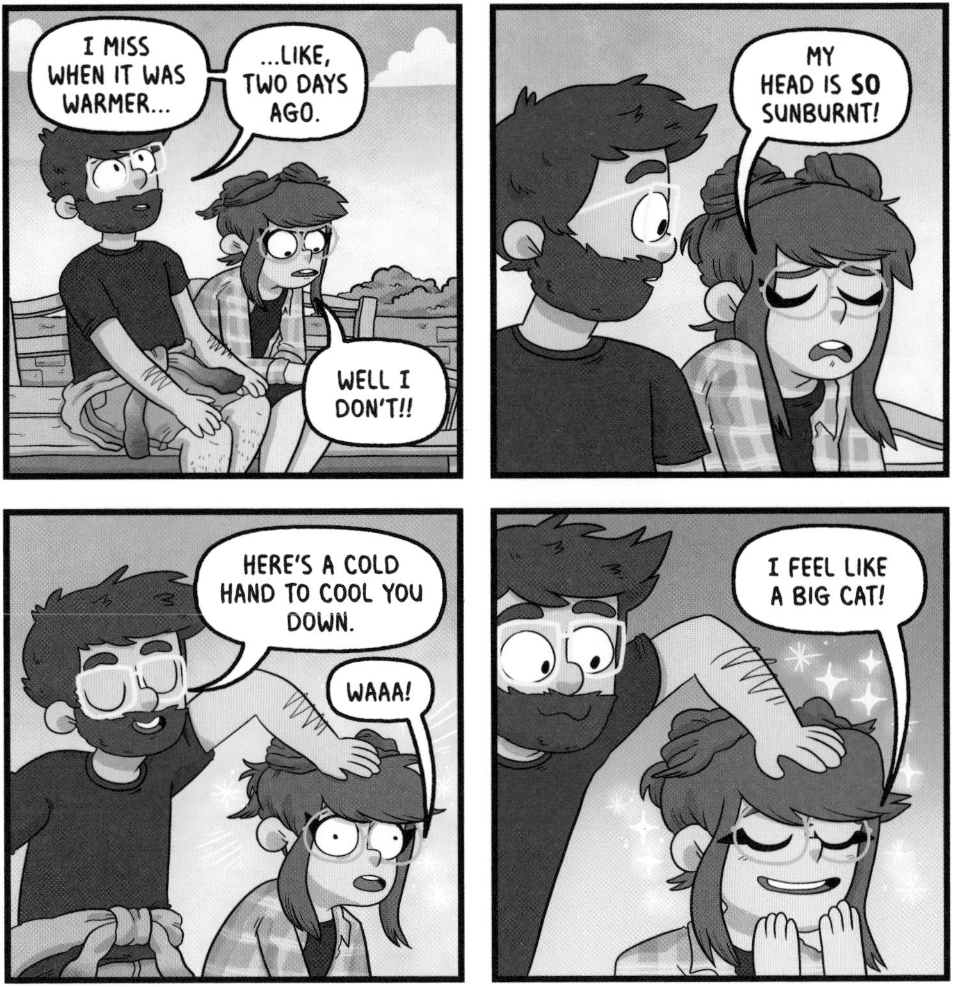
I MISS WHEN IT WAS WARMER...
...LIKE, TWO DAYS AGO.
WELL I DON'T!!
MY HEAD IS **SO** SUNBURNT!
HERE'S A COLD HAND TO COOL YOU DOWN.
WAAA!
I FEEL LIKE A BIG CAT!

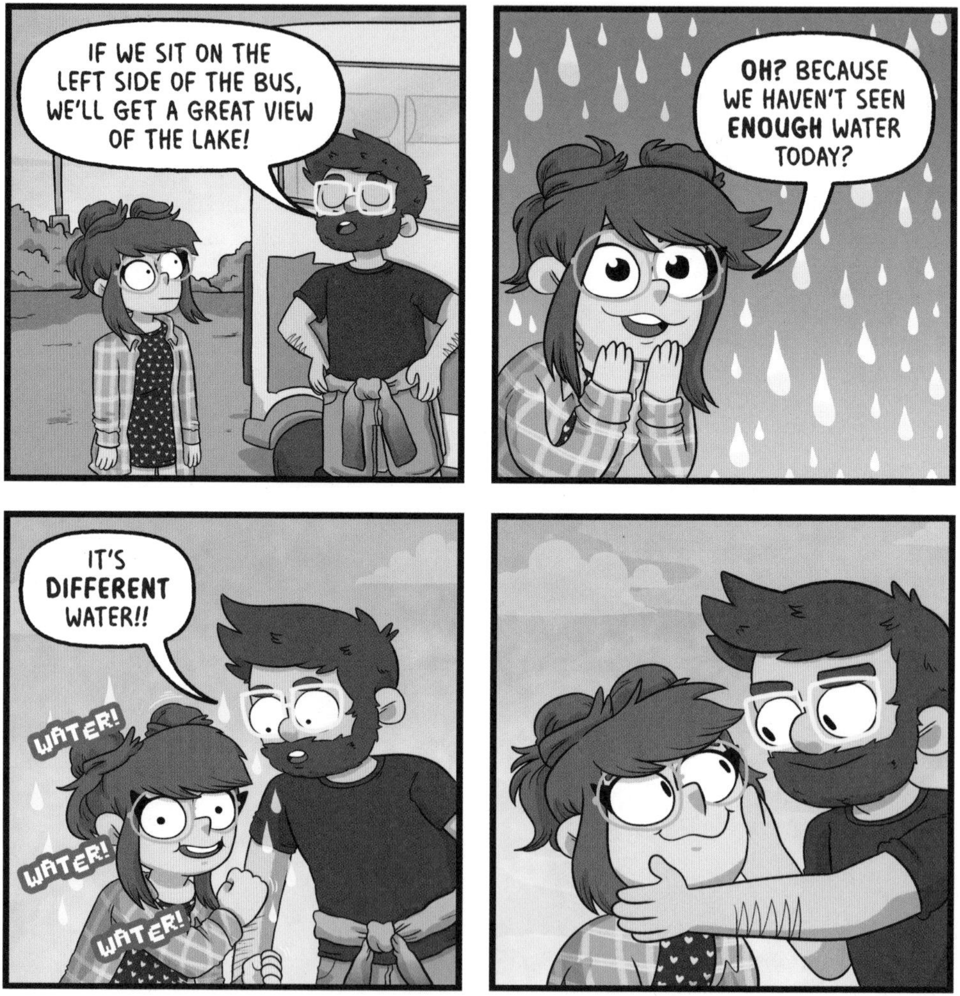
IF WE SIT ON THE LEFT SIDE OF THE BUS, WE'LL GET A GREAT VIEW OF THE LAKE!
OH? BECAUSE WE HAVEN'T SEEN ENOUGH WATER TODAY?
IT'S DIFFERENT WATER!!
WATER!
WATER!
WATER!

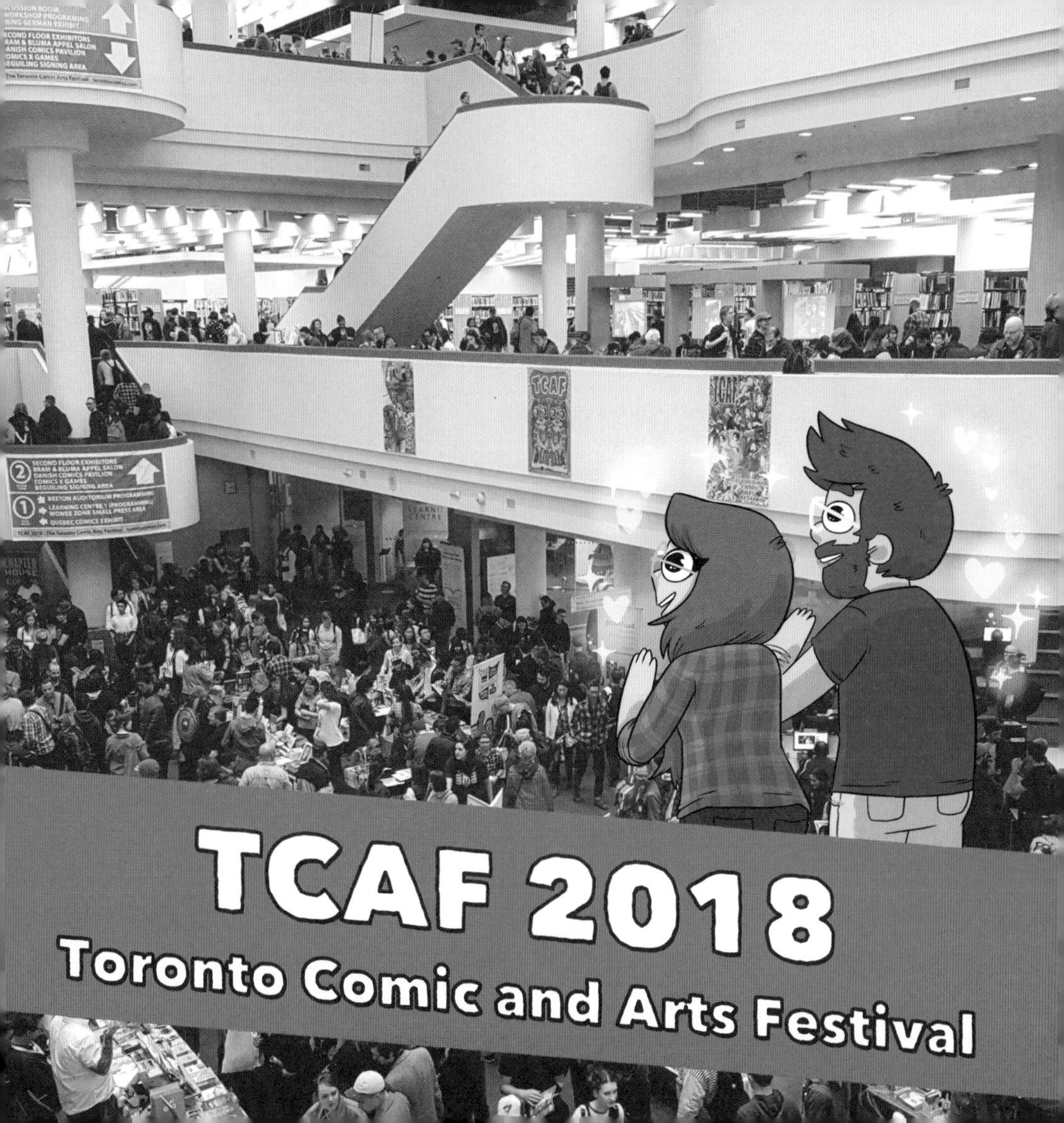
SECOND FLOOR EXHIBITORS
BRAM & BLUMA APPEL SALON
DANISH COMICS PAVILION
COMICS X GAMES
BEGUILING SIGNING AREA
BEETON AUDITORIUM PROGRAMMING
LEARNING CENTRE 1 (PROGRAMMING)
WOWEE ZONK SMALL PRESS AREA
QUEBEC COMICS EXHIBIT
TCAF 2018
Toronto Comic and Arts Festival

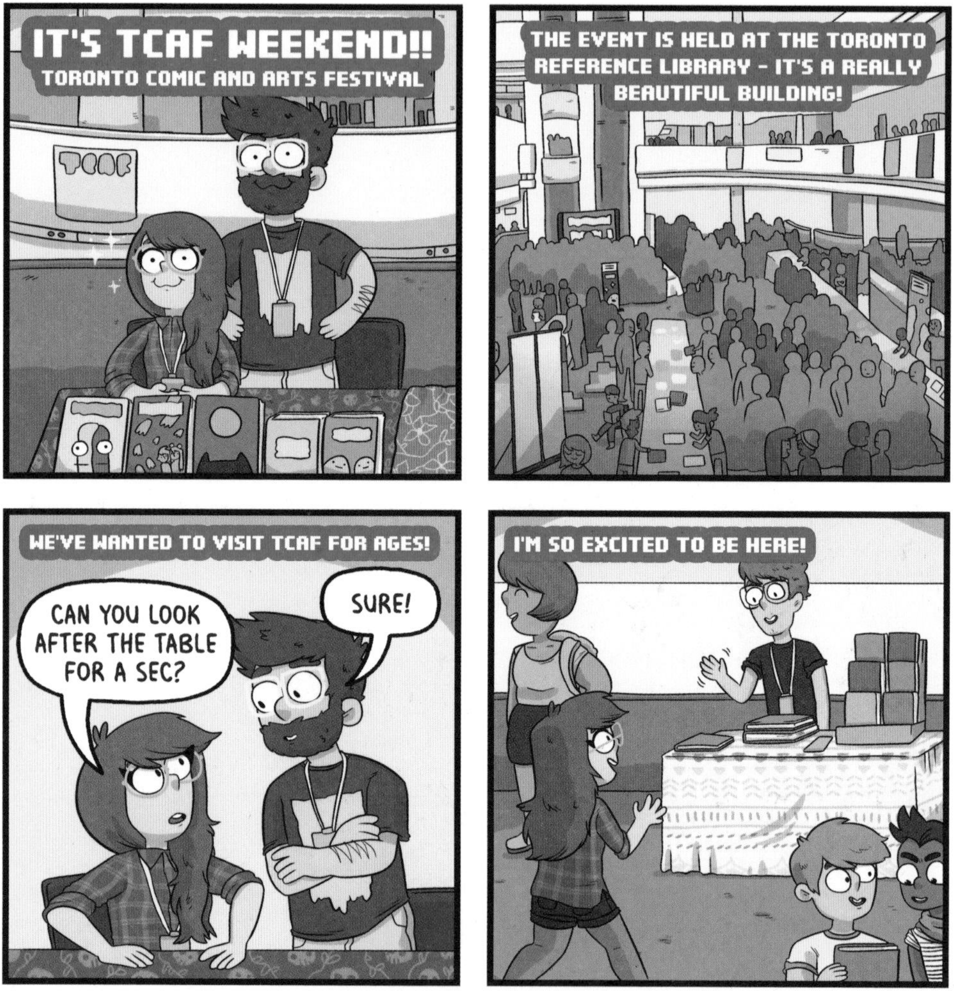
IT'S TCAF WEEKEND!!
TORONTO COMIC AND ARTS FESTIVAL
TCAF
THE EVENT IS HELD AT THE TORONTO REFERENCE LIBRARY - IT'S A REALLY BEAUTIFUL BUILDING!
WE'VE WANTED TO VISIT TCAF FOR AGES!
CAN YOU LOOK AFTER THE TABLE FOR A SEC?
SURE!
I'M SO EXCITED TO BE HERE!

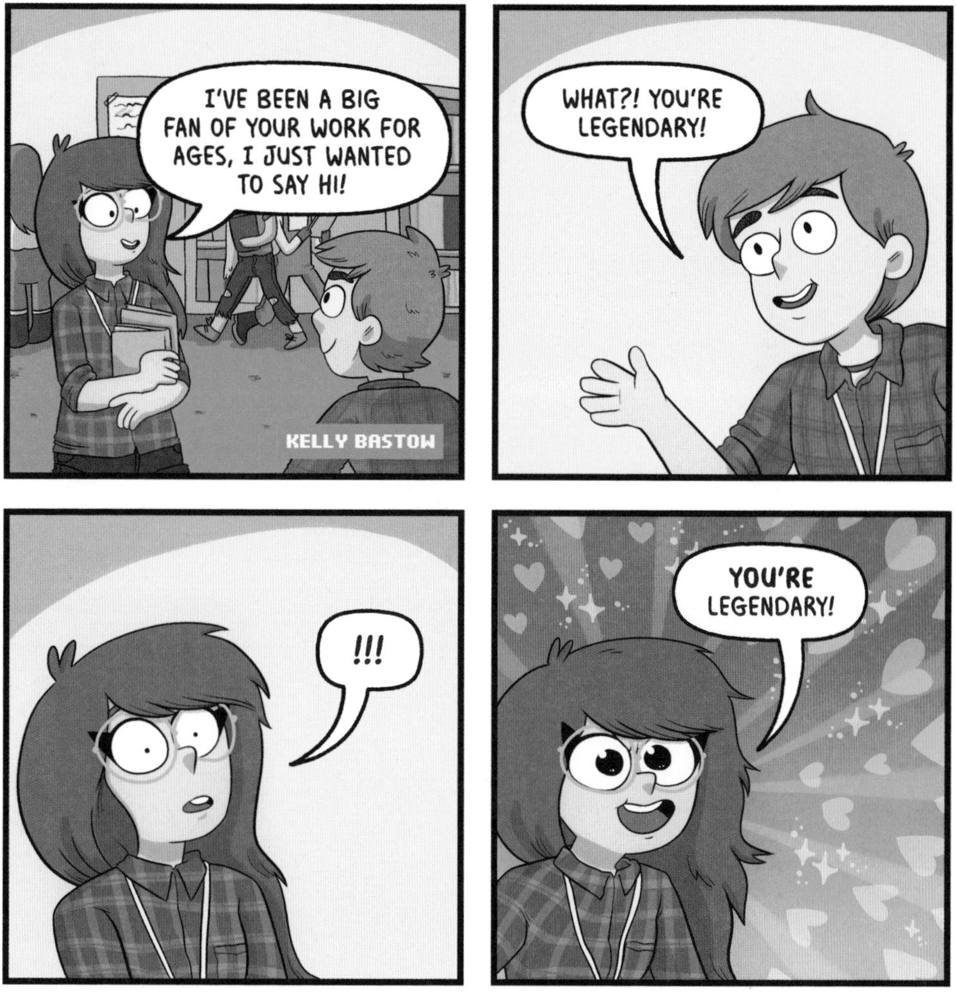
I'VE BEEN A BIG FAN OF YOUR WORK FOR AGES, I JUST WANTED TO SAY HI!
KELLY BASTOW
WHAT?! YOU'RE LEGENDARY!
!!!
YOU'RE LEGENDARY!

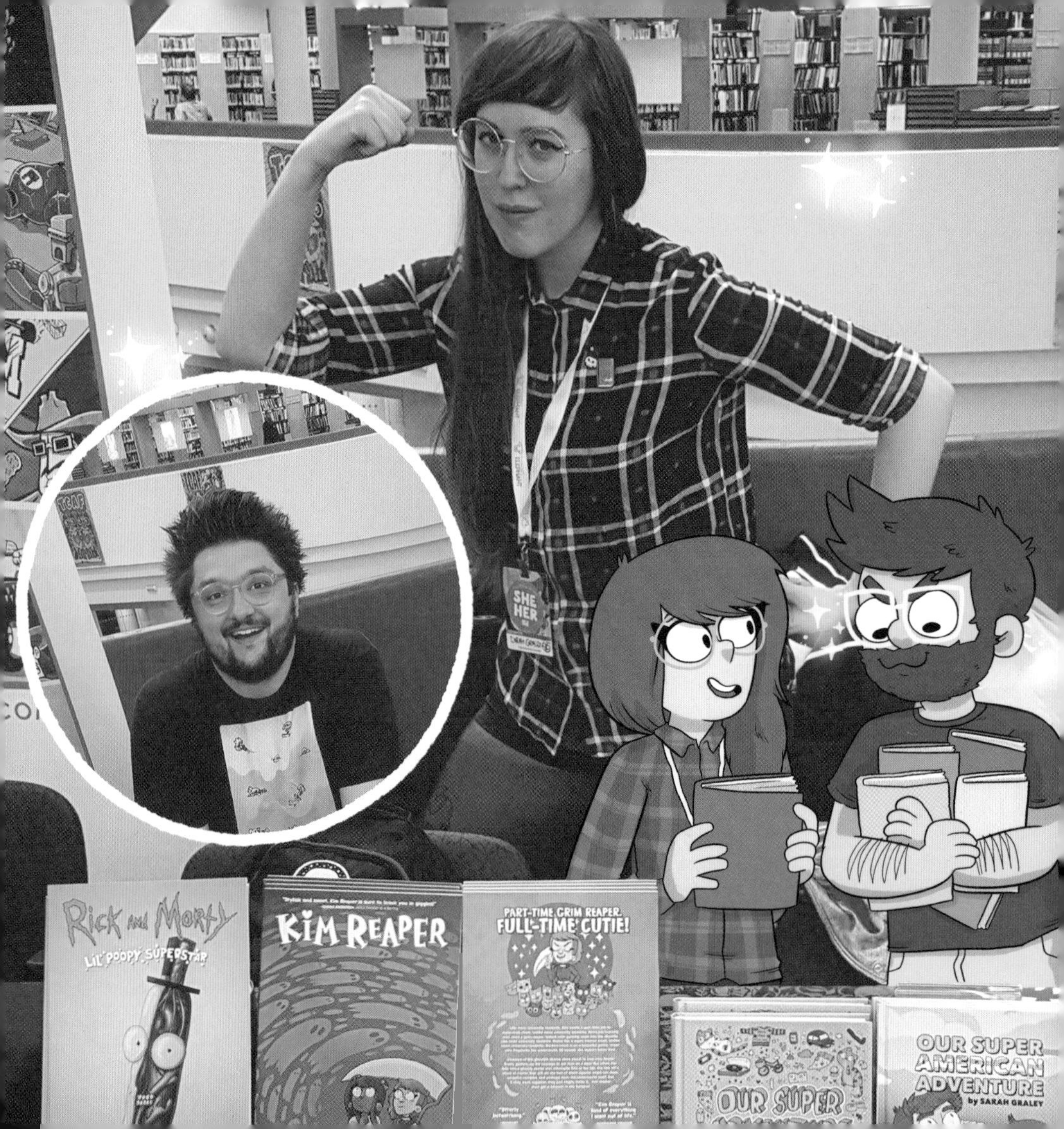
SHE
HER
Rick and Morty
LIL' POOPY SUPERSTAR
KIM REAPER
PART-TIME GRIM REAPER, FULL-TIME CUTIE!
OUR SUPER
OUR SUPER AMERICAN ADVENTURE
by SARAH GRALEY

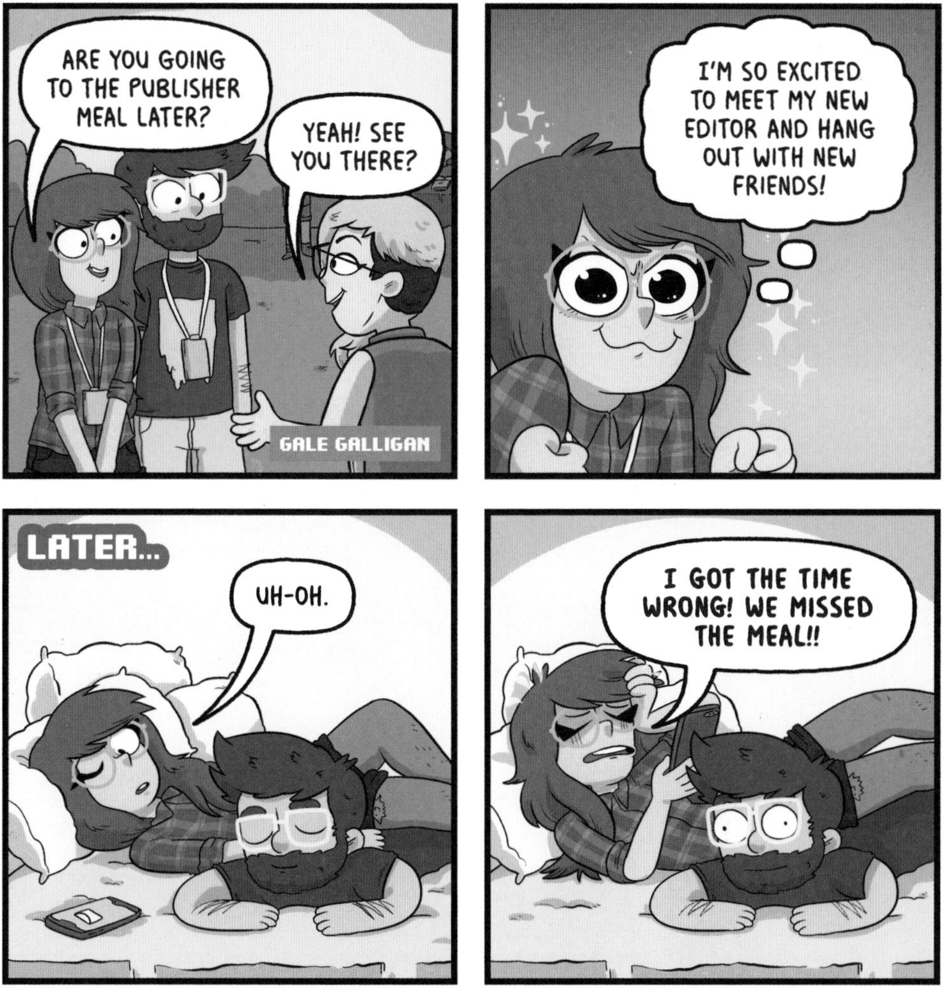
ARE YOU GOING TO THE PUBLISHER MEAL LATER?
YEAH! SEE YOU THERE?
GALE GALLIGAN
I'M SO EXCITED TO MEET MY NEW EDITOR AND HANG OUT WITH NEW FRIENDS!
LATER...
UH-OH.
I GOT THE TIME WRONG! WE MISSED THE MEAL!!

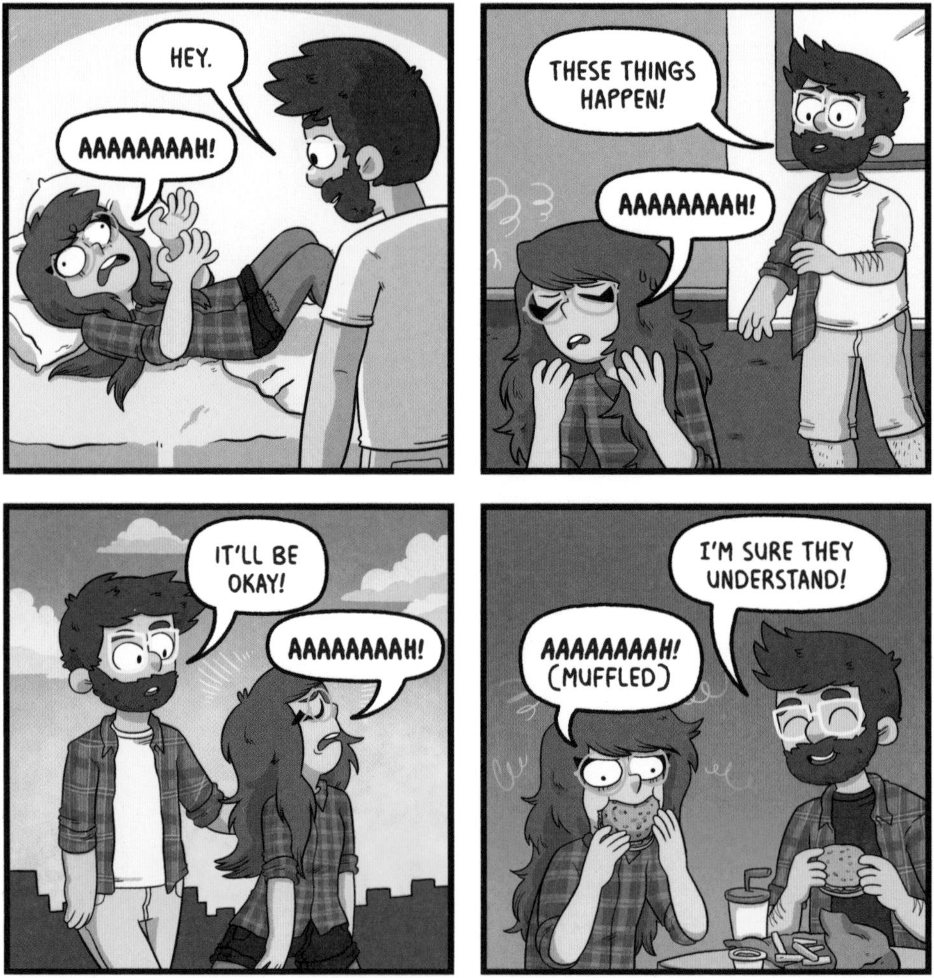
HEY.
AAAAAAAAH!
THESE THINGS HAPPEN!
AAAAAAAAH!
IT'LL BE OKAY!
AAAAAAAAH!
I'M SURE THEY UNDERSTAND!
AAAAAAAAH! (MUFFLED)

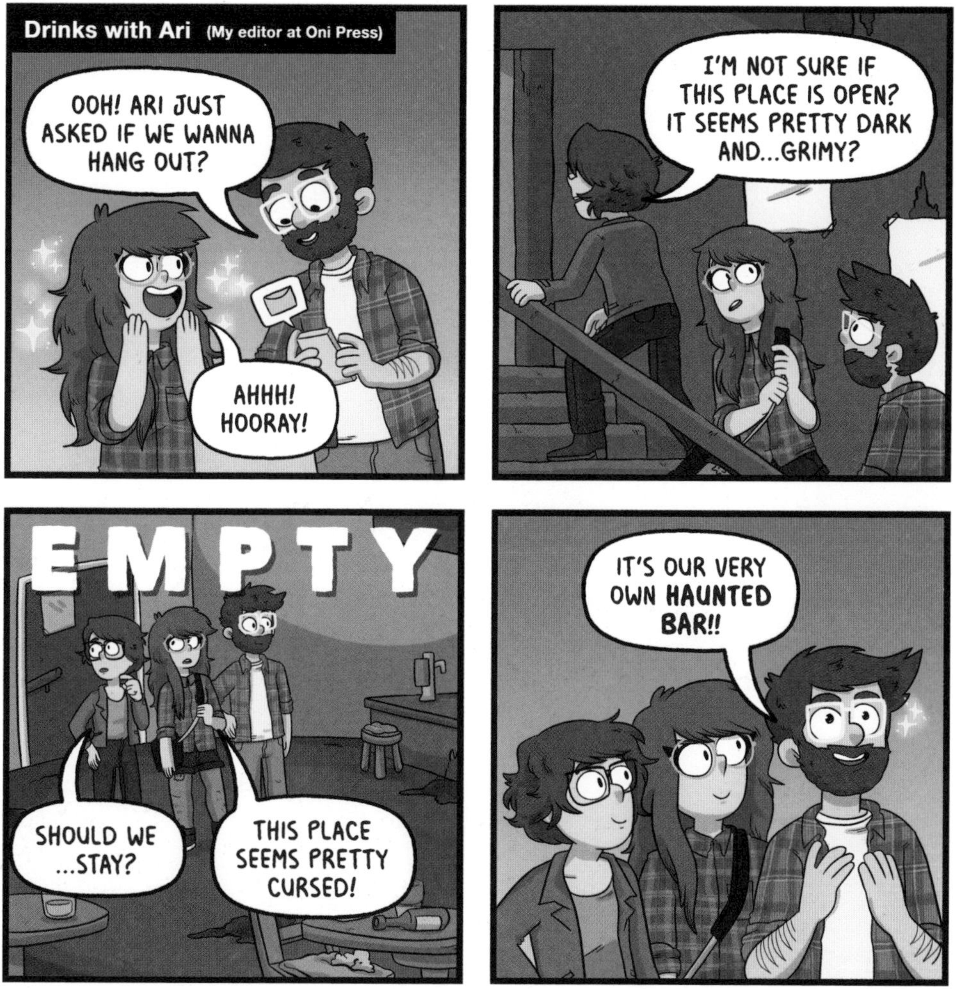
Drinks with Ari (My editor at Oni Press)
OOH! ARI JUST ASKED IF WE WANNA HANG OUT?
AHHH! HOORAY!
I'M NOT SURE IF THIS PLACE IS OPEN? IT SEEMS PRETTY DARK AND...GRIMY?
EMPTY
SHOULD WE ...STAY?
THIS PLACE SEEMS PRETTY CURSED!
IT'S OUR VERY OWN **HAUNTED BAR!!**

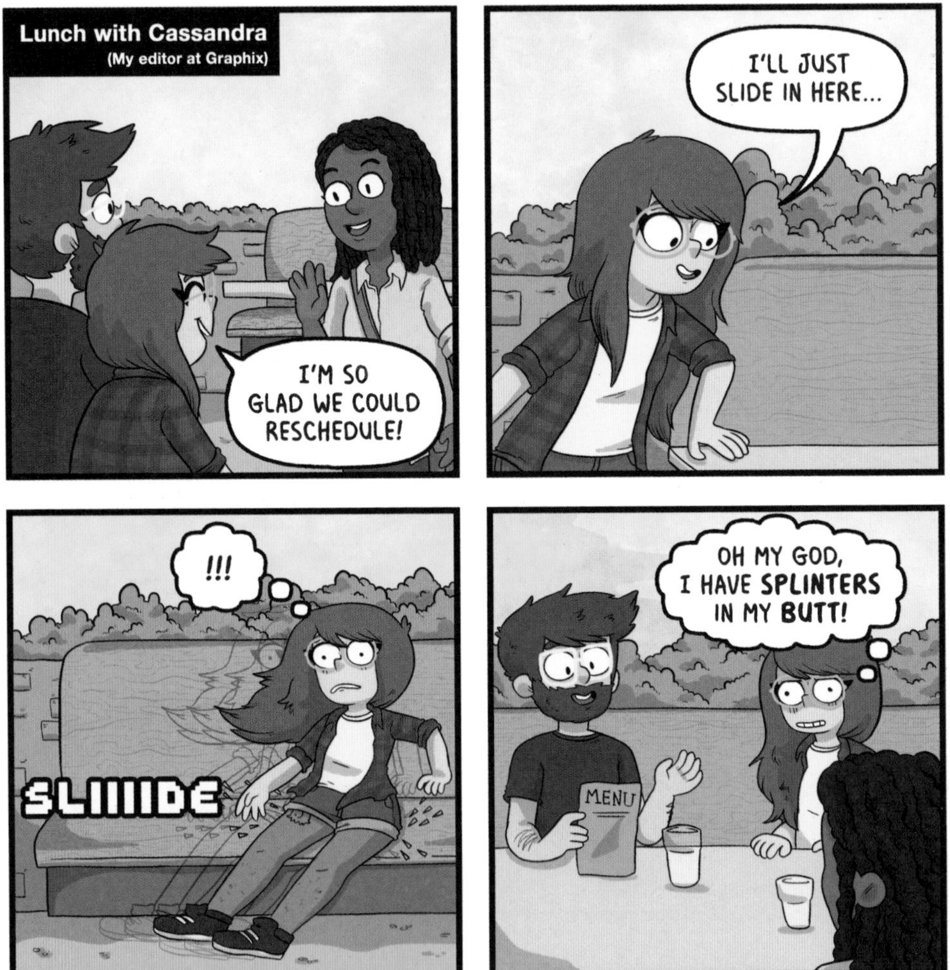
Lunch with Cassandra
(My editor at Graphix)
I'M SO GLAD WE COULD RESCHEDULE!
I'LL JUST SLIDE IN HERE...
!!!
SLIIIIDE
OH MY GOD, I HAVE SPLINTERS IN MY BUTT!
MENU

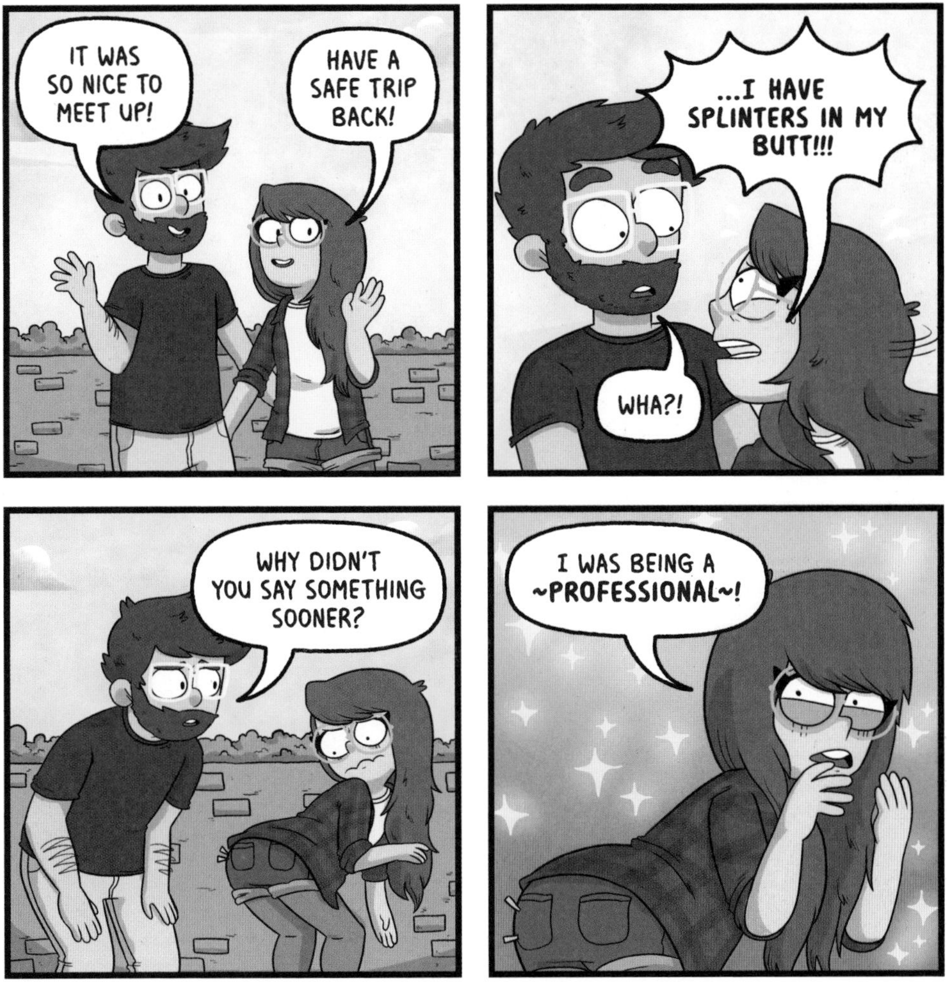
IT WAS SO NICE TO MEET UP!
HAVE A SAFE TRIP BACK!
...I HAVE SPLINTERS IN MY BUTT!!!
WHA?!
WHY DIDN'T YOU SAY SOMETHING SOONER?
I WAS BEING A ~PROFESSIONAL~!

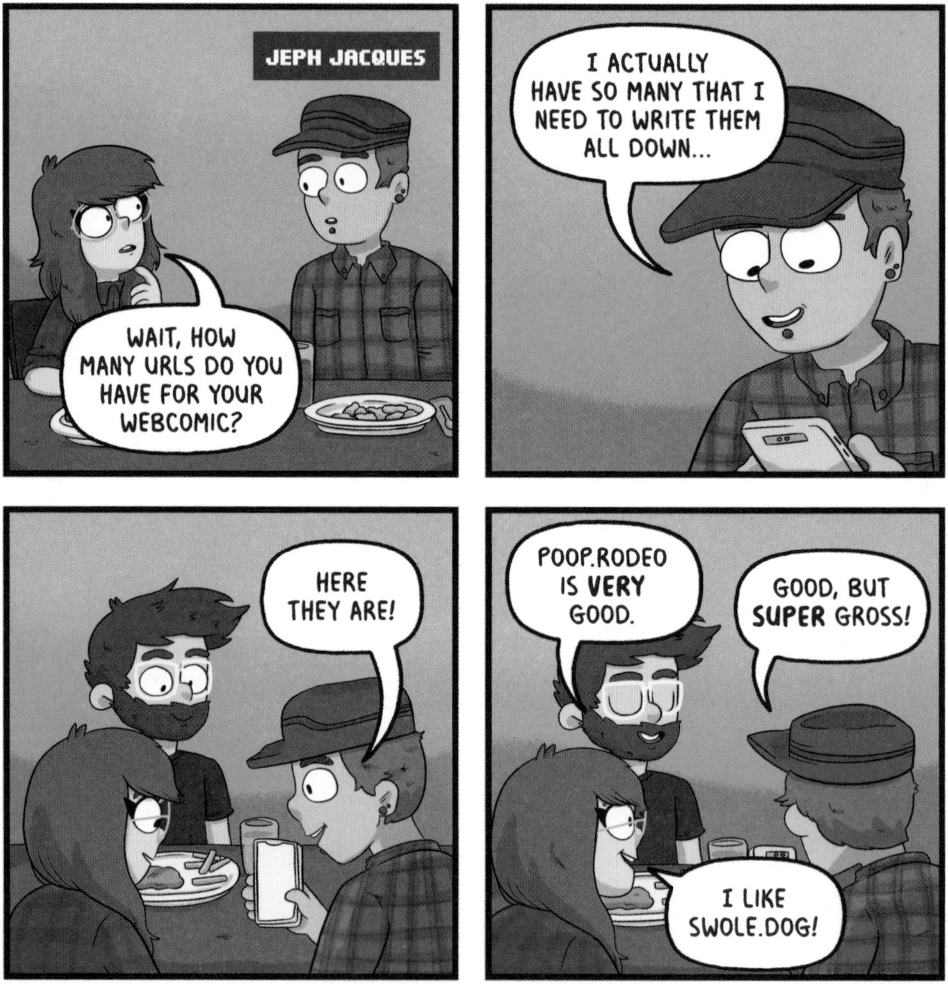
JEPH JACQUES
WAIT, HOW MANY URLS DO YOU HAVE FOR YOUR WEBCOMIC?
I ACTUALLY HAVE SO MANY THAT I NEED TO WRITE THEM ALL DOWN...
HERE THEY ARE!
POOP.RODEO IS **VERY** GOOD.
GOOD, BUT **SUPER** GROSS!
I LIKE SWOLE.DOG!

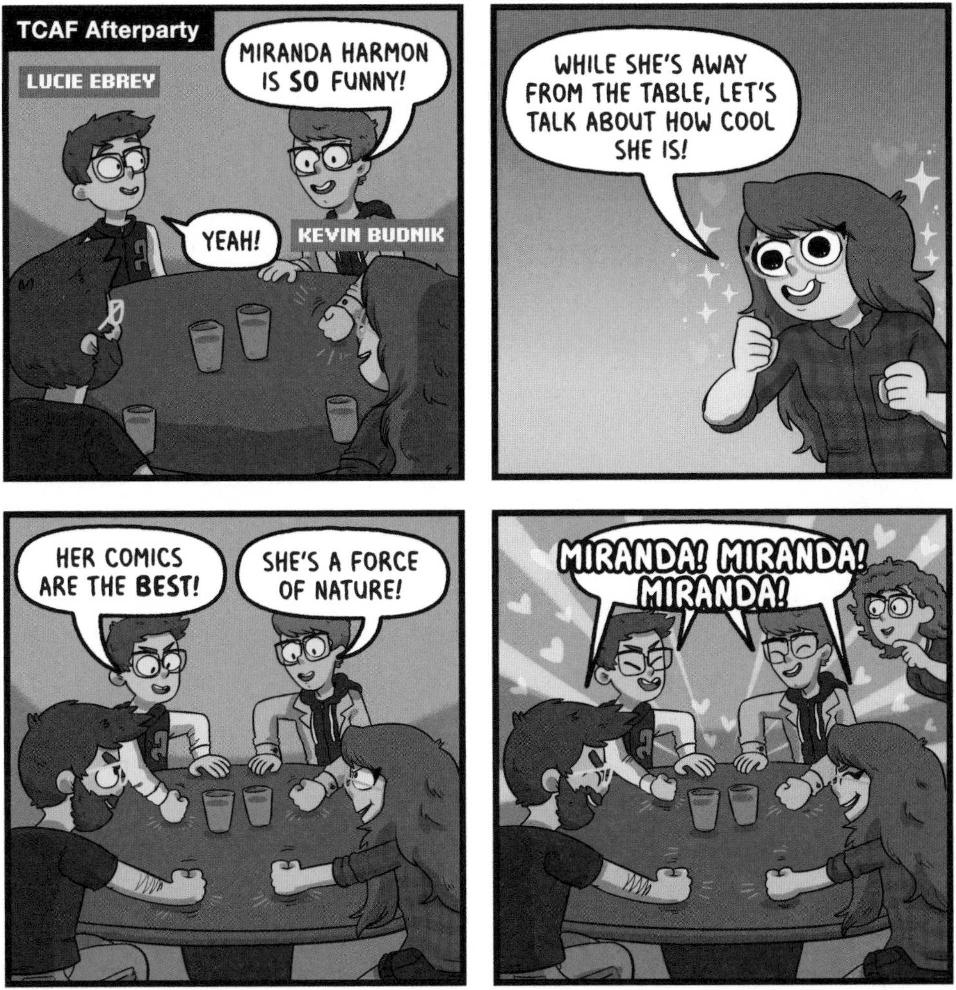
TCAF Afterparty
LUCIE EBREY
MIRANDA HARMON IS SO FUNNY!
YEAH!
KEVIN BUDNIK
WHILE SHE'S AWAY FROM THE TABLE, LET'S TALK ABOUT HOW COOL SHE IS!
HER COMICS ARE THE BEST!
SHE'S A FORCE OF NATURE!
MIRANDA! MIRANDA! MIRANDA!

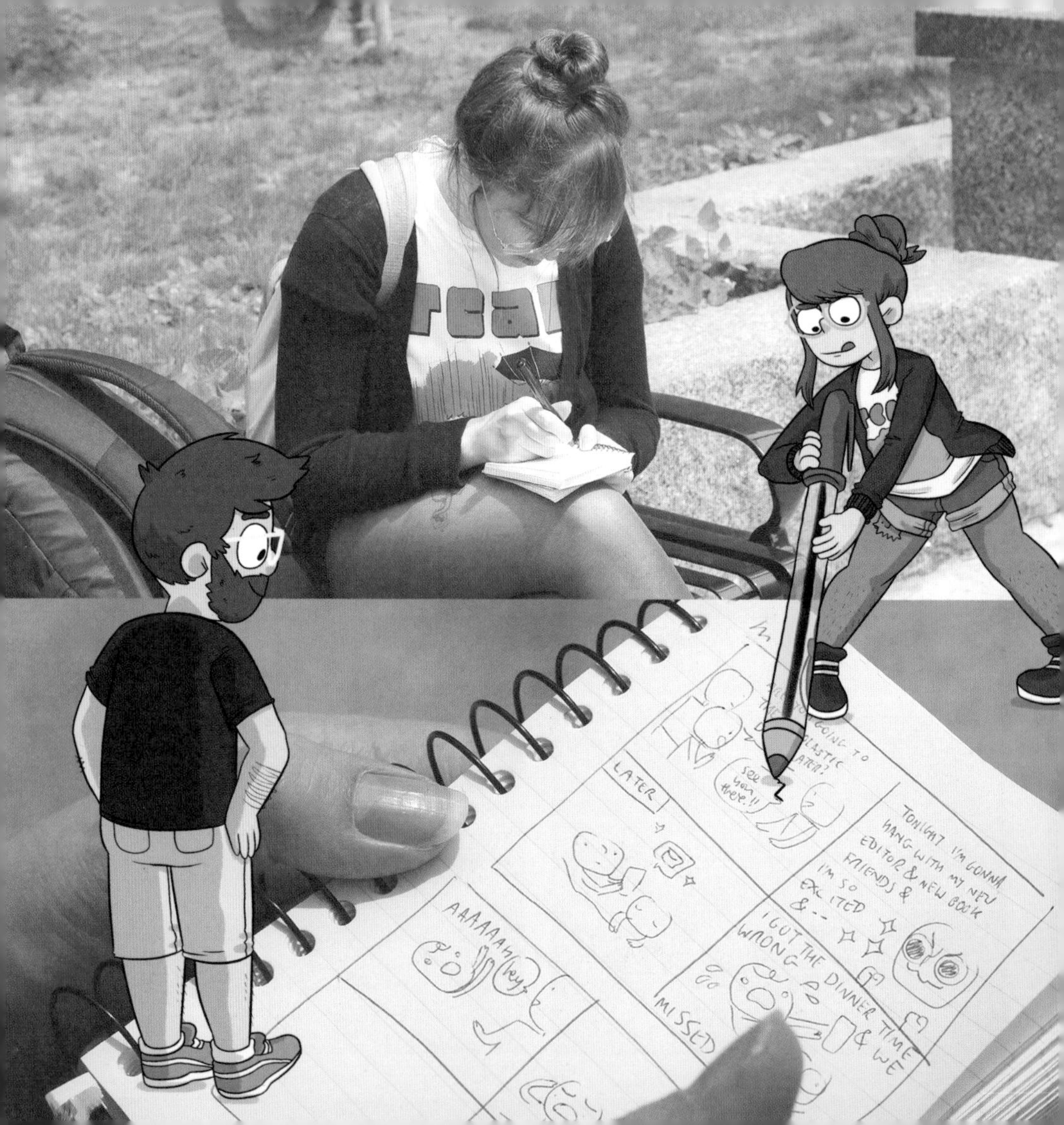

TONIGHT I'M GONNA HANG WITH MY NEW EDITOR & NEW BOOK FRIENDS & I'M SO EXCITED & --
See you there!!
LATER
I GOT THE DINNER TIME WRONG & WE
MISSED
AAAAAAAH
hey

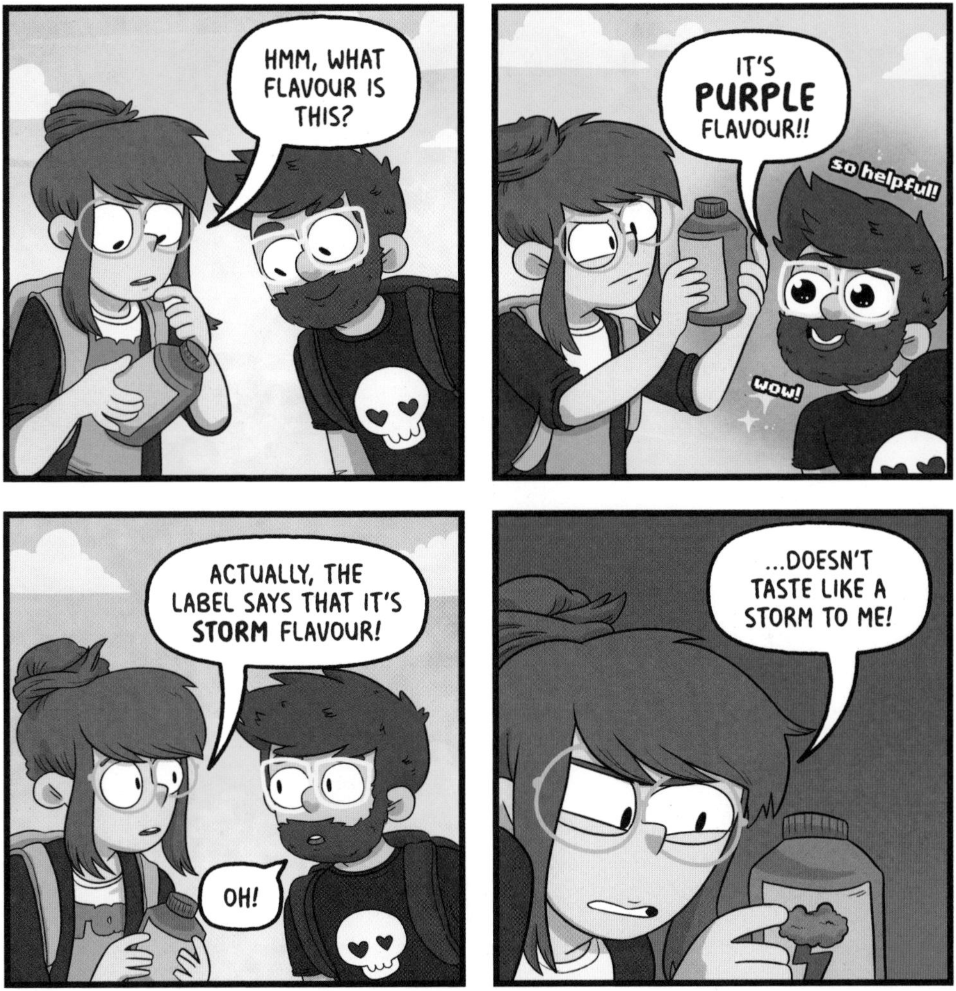
HMM, WHAT FLAVOUR IS THIS?
IT'S PURPLE FLAVOUR!!
so helpful!
wow!
ACTUALLY, THE LABEL SAYS THAT IT'S STORM FLAVOUR!
OH!
...DOESN'T TASTE LIKE A STORM TO ME!

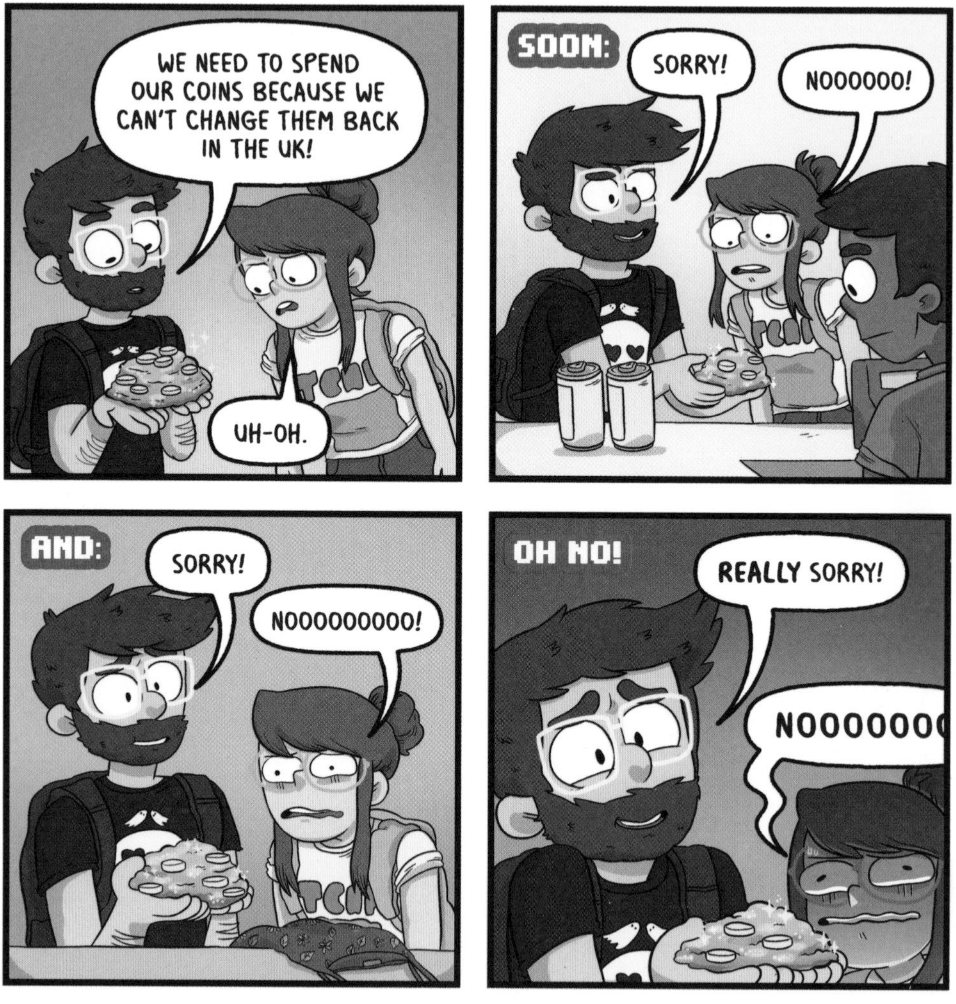
WE NEED TO SPEND OUR COINS BECAUSE WE CAN'T CHANGE THEM BACK IN THE UK!
UH-OH.
SOON:
SORRY!
NOOOOOO!
AND:
SORRY!
NOOOOOOOOO!
OH NO!
REALLY SORRY!
NOOOOOOO

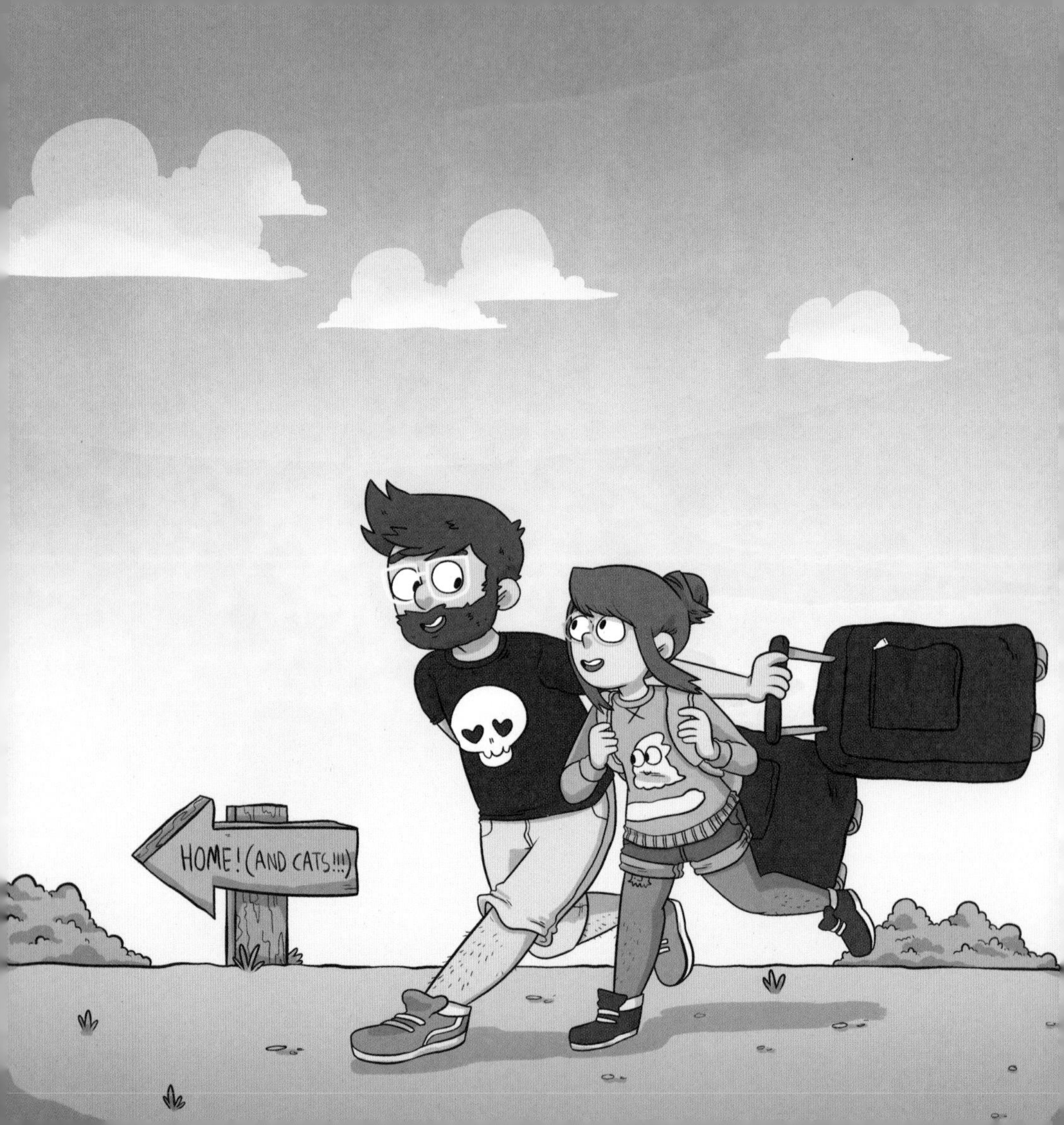
HOME! (AND CATS!!!)

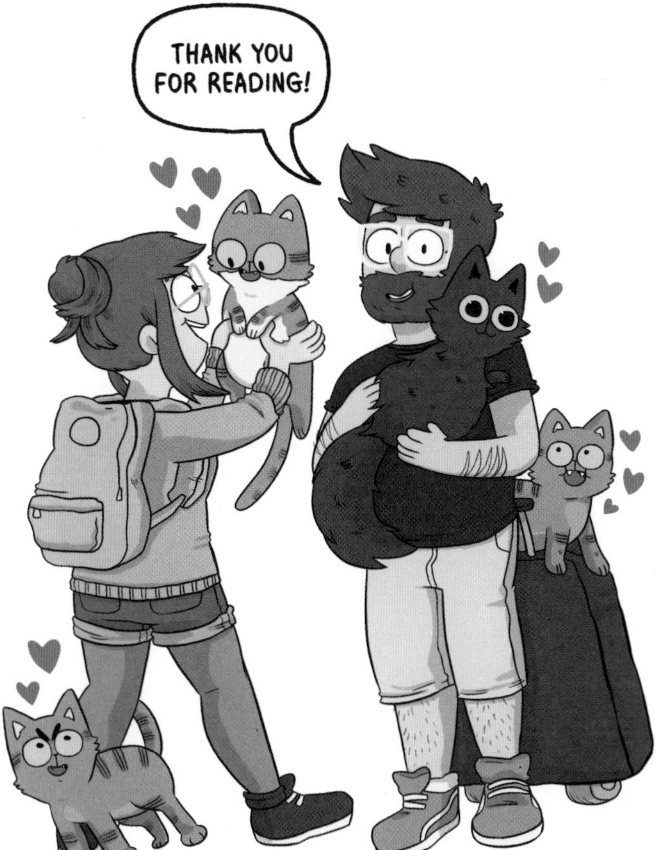
THANK YOU FOR READING!

THE SUPER ADVENTURERS

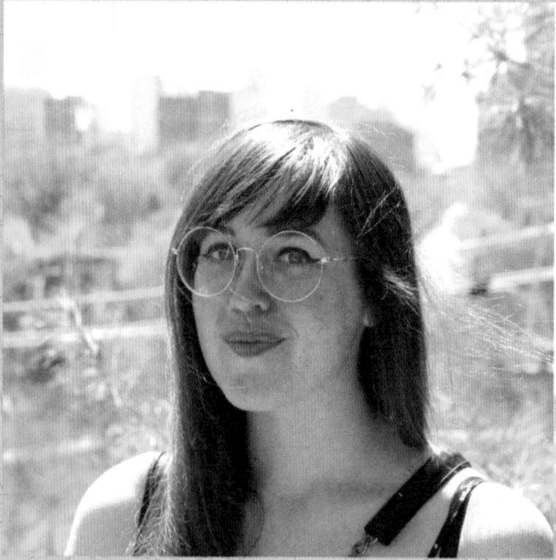

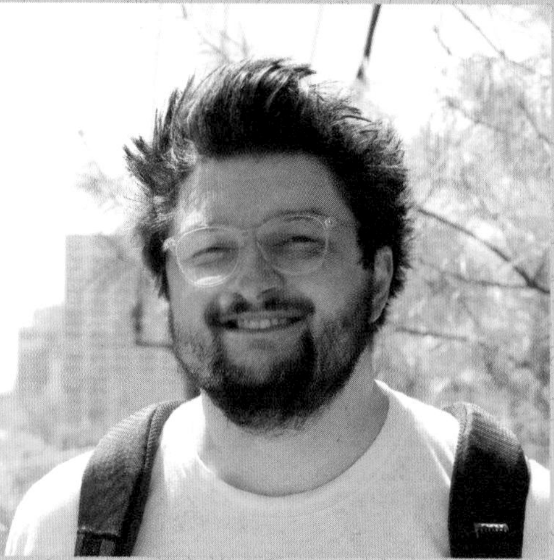

Sarah Graley is a comic writer and artist who lives in Birmingham, UK, with four cats and a cat-like boy! She has been drawing *Our Super Adventure* since 2012, alongside other comics such as *Kim Reaper* (Oni Press), *Rick and Morty: Lil' Poopy Superstar* (Oni Press), *Glitch* (Scholastic Graphix) and *Minecraft: Volume One* (Dark Horse Comics). She's currently making a book called *Donut the Destroyer* with Stef!

You can find out more about her at **sarahgraley.com**!

Stef Purenins is a cat-like boy who does lettering and colour assisting, as well as helping Sarah out with design and admin and other behind-the-scenes stuff! He's currently making a book called *Donut the Destroyer* with Sarah!

THE SUPER ADVENTURERS

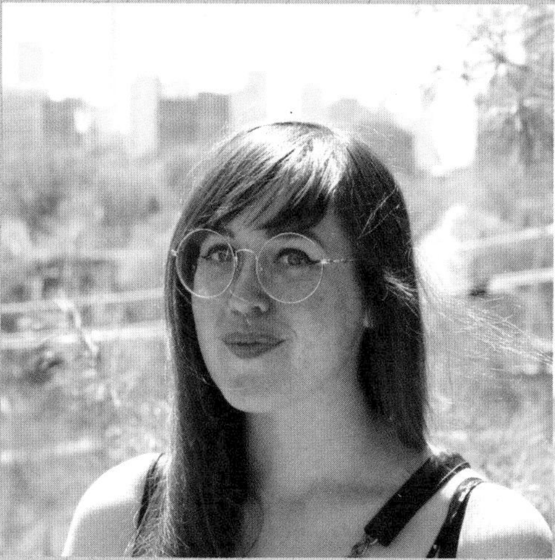

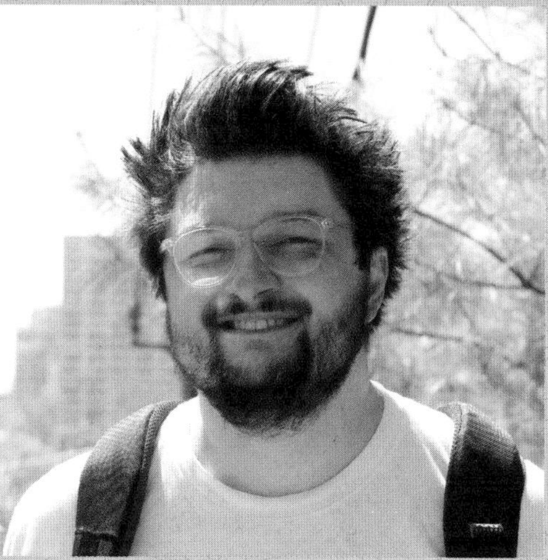

Sarah Graley is a comic writer and artist who lives in Birmingham, UK, with four cats and a cat-like boy! She has been drawing *Our Super Adventure* since 2012, alongside other comics such as *Kim Reaper* (Oni Press), *Rick and Morty: Lil' Poopy Superstar* (Oni Press), *Glitch* (Scholastic Graphix) and *Minecraft: Volume One* (Dark Horse Comics). She's currently making a book called *Donut the Destroyer* with Stef!

You can find out more about her at **sarahgraley.com**!

Stef Purenins is a cat-like boy who does lettering and colour assisting, as well as helping Sarah out with design and admin and other behind-the-scenes stuff! He's currently making a book called *Donut the Destroyer* with Sarah!

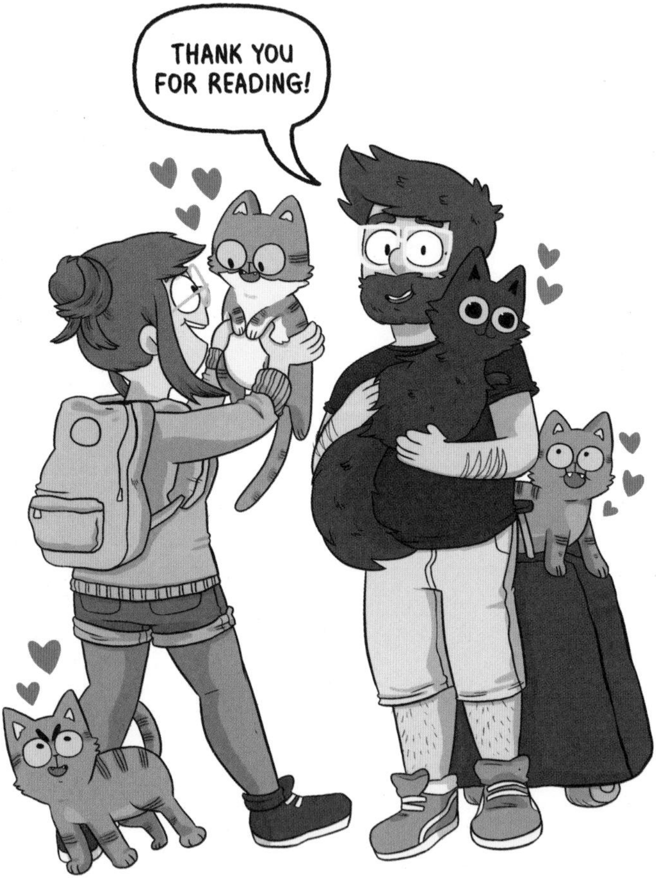
THANK YOU FOR READING!

FIND US ONLINE

sarahgraley.com
oursuperadventure.com
@sarahgraleyart & @tinyspells
facebook.com/sarahgraleyart
instagram.com/sarahgraley
sonicthecomic.bandcamp.com

READ MORE OUR SUPER ADVENTURE!

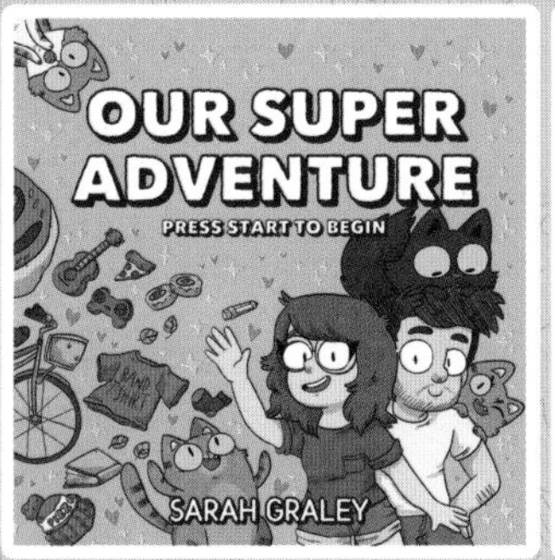
OUR SUPER ADVENTURE
PRESS START TO BEGIN
SARAH GRALEY

Our Super Adventure: Press Start To Begin

The first volume of diary comics! Contains 200 comics all about cats, pizza, and navigating adult life!

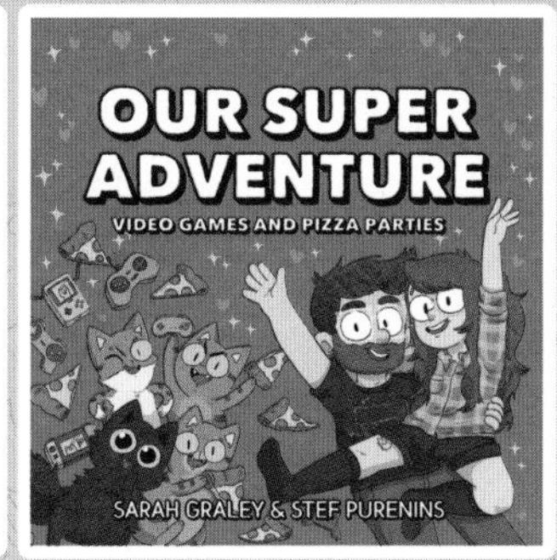
OUR SUPER ADVENTURE
VIDEO GAMES AND PIZZA PARTIES
SARAH GRALEY & STEF PURENINS

Our Super Adventure: Video Games and Pizza Parties

The second volume! Collects another 200 comics from between 2015 and 2018! More video games! More pizza! MORE CATS!

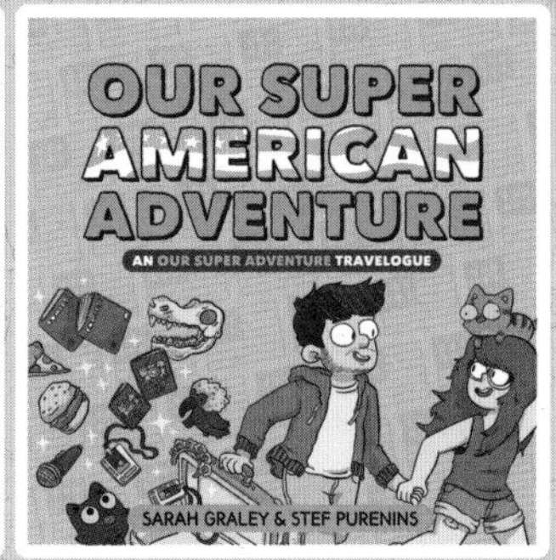
OUR SUPER AMERICAN ADVENTURE
AN OUR SUPER ADVENTURE TRAVELOGUE
SARAH GRALEY & STEF PURENINS

Our Super American Adventure

Travel comics all about our trip to America! We visited LA, San Diego Comic-Con, and New York!

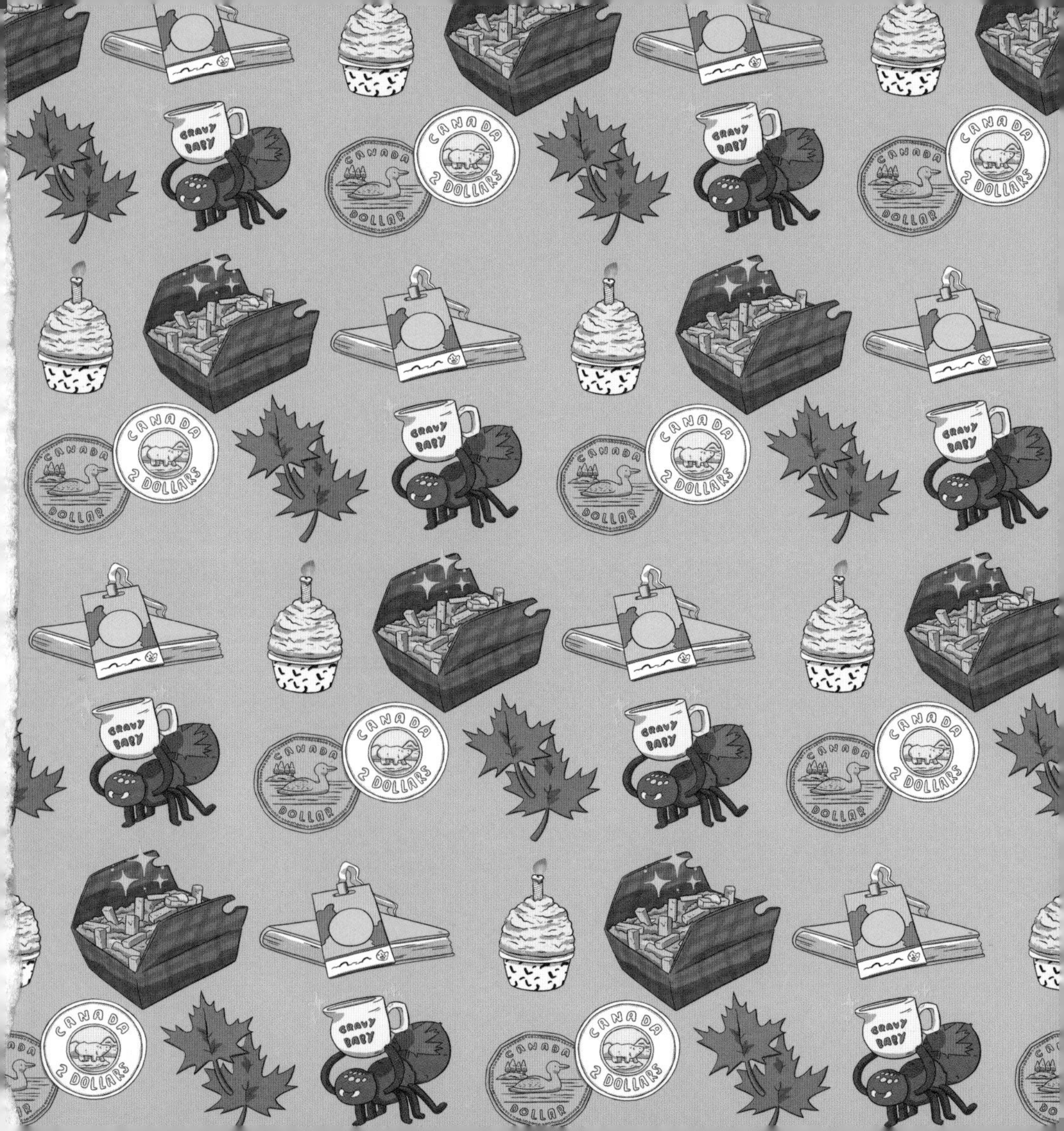
GRAVY BABY
CANADA
2 DOLLARS
CANADA
DOLLAR

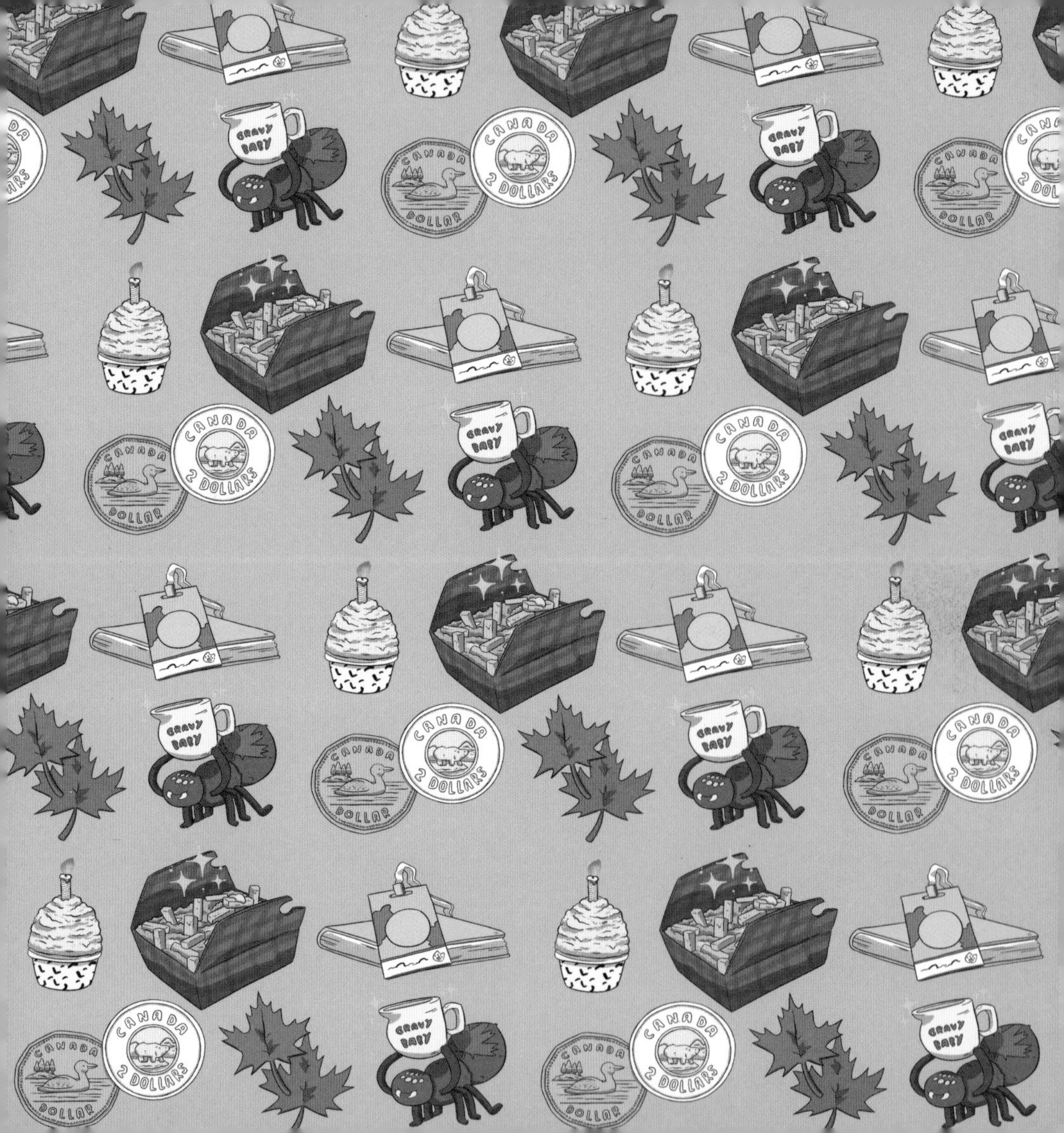
GRAVY BABY
CANADA
DOLLAR
CANADA
2 DOLLARS